Secrets to Noncompetitive Government Contract

Printed in the United States of America

First Printed, 2019

ISBN: 9781796402483

Integrity Lion Acquisitions, LLC
9109 Athens Drive
Argyle, TX 76226

www.integritylionacq.com

Secrets to Noncompetitive Government Contracts

Robert Wink, PMP, CFCM

Integrity Lion
Acquisitions, LLC

2019

TABLE OF CONTENTS

Introduction

Every business is trying to increase sales, and revenue; which will result in accolades and profit. There are three industries to sell to:

- **Consumer** – Business to consumer, (B2C), refers to the transactions conducted directly between a company and consumers who are the end-users of its products or services. The business to consumer as a business model differs significantly from the business-to-business model, which refers to commerce between two or more businesses.

- **Business** – Business to business, (B2B), is a form of transaction between businesses, such as one involving a manufacturer and wholesaler, or a wholesaler and a retailer. Business to business refers to business that is conducted between companies, rather than between a company and individual consumers.

- **Government** – Business-to-Government, (B2G), refers to business conducted between private sector firms and Governments.

Selling to the Government is not as easy as picking up the phone and asking the Government to buy your product or door to door sales or even selling to a business. Whereas a consumer or business has the right to purchase from anyone they decide. Regardless of price, quality, or even where the product is made. This type of purchasing is allowed due to the Competition Law also known as the Anti-Trust Law; which has three elements:

1. Prohibiting agreements or practices that restrict free trading and competition between businesses. This includes in particular the repression of free trade caused by cartels.

2. Banning abusive behavior by a firm dominating a market, or anti-competitive practices that tend to lead to such a dominant position. Practices controlled in this way may include predatory pricing, tying, price gouging, refusal to deal, and many others.

3. Supervising the mergers and acquisitions of large corporations, including some joint ventures. Transactions that are considered to threaten the competitive process can be prohibited altogether, or approved subject to "remedies" such as an obligation to divest part of the merged business or to offer licenses or access to facilities to enable other businesses to continue competing.

Substance and practice of competition law varies from jurisdiction to jurisdiction. Protecting the interests of consumers (consumer welfare) and ensuring that entrepreneurs have an opportunity to compete in the market economy are often treated as important objectives. Competition law is closely connected with law on deregulation of access to markets, state aids and subsidies, the privatization of state-owned assets and the establishment of independent sector regulators, among other market-oriented supply-side policies. In recent decades, competition law has been viewed to provide better public services.

The Federal Acquisition Regulation (FAR) and the supplements of each agency govern the federal Procurement Process. The FAR and supplements can be found at www.acquisition.gov & http://farsite.hill.af.mil/ this book will have some heavy FAR parts, but it is imperative that as a business to know where to research this information.

The United States Government published the Competition in Contracting Act (CICA); which was established by Congress in 1984 to encourage and create competition for Government Contracts. The theory behind this Act is that increased competition will result in improved savings to the Government and Tax Payer through competitive pricing. The CICA provides for full and open competition in the awarding of Government contracts.

Unless the Full and Open Competition has restriction that are mandated by the FAR for the vendor to be registered in www.sam.gov, and have specific small business set-aside. CICA mandates that any contract expected to be greater than $25,000 must be advertised at least 15 days prior to bid solicitation (there is an exception to this rule). This advertising is intended to increase the number of bidders competing for Government contracts, thereby allowing for full and open competition. CICA required the Government to follow these procedures with limited exceptions; any departure from CICA must be documented and approved by the appropriate Government official.

This book will educate you on the exceptions to the Competition in Contracting Act that are legal. Those exceptions are legal due to the Federal Acquisition Regulation and the supplements from each Government Agency. It will also uncover how the Government does business from the Fiscal Triad, Market Research, Back Room Deals (Illegal), Ethical Violations, the tricks to Set-Asides, Unsolicited Proposals, and Other Than Full and Open Competition also known as sole source contracts. FAR Subpart 8 – Limited Source Justification will not be reviewed in this book.

How to write for the Requiring Activities Justification and Approval for the sole source and what the Contracting Officer shall determine to award the contract to your company, Fair & Reasonable & Determination of Responsibility.

And finally closing remarks.

Chapter 1 - Separation of Powers/Positions – The Fiscal Triad

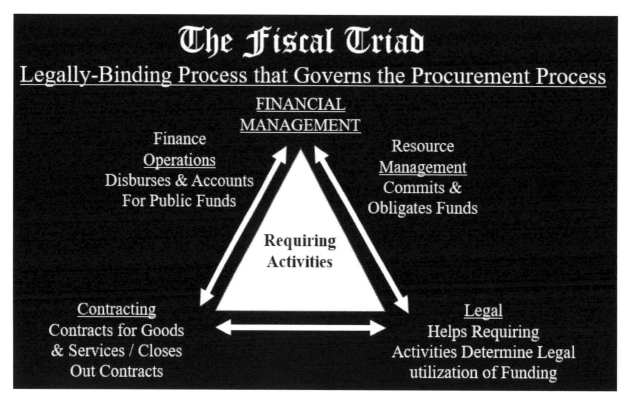

The Fiscal Triad depicted illustrates the legally-binding process that governs the critical

path between contracting and acquisition management, internal controls, and fiscal law (legal)

prescribed for the procurement process. Contracting and legal counsel comprise a system that

fulfills the full spectrum of required fiscal support, from the acquisition and certification of funds, to the legal review of the proposed contracting action, to the contracting for goods and services, and finally to the disbursing and accounting of public funds (your tax dollars). At the center of the Fiscal Triad is the "requiring activity" whom develops the requirement from supplies, services, and construction projects. The requiring activity develops the requirement and initiates the process.

All elements of the Fiscal Triad must coordinate to conform to existing policies, regulations, and laws to prevent fraud, waste and abuse of Government funds. To ensure separation of duties, each element of the triad is independent, yet each element works closely with the other to obtain products or services to meet the requiring activities needs in compliance with applicable laws and regulations.

Let's Simplify that

Requiring Activity – Can be an individual or a program office that is responsible for establishing the agencies need. The agencies need can be a supply, service to be performed, or a construction project. The requiring activity is the one that will develop the documentation needed for this requirement that the Government intends to purchase.

Financial Management Team – relates to planning, directing, monitoring, organizing, and controlling an entity's financial resources in an efficient and effective manner. The financial management team can consist of multiple positions, but the two important positions are the Finance Operations and Resource Manager.

- Finance Operations – The execution of the joint finance mission to provide financial advice and guidance, support of the procurement process, providing pay support, and providing disbursing support by monitoring the accounts payable sub ledger, analyzes the monthly budget to actual numbers and compiles information for budget preparation, external audits and other projects. Disburses and accounts of public funds.

- Resource Manager – Commits and Obligates Funds. Resource Managers are usually over offices that control the budget. They make sure that each cent is accounted for and is in the best interest of the Government. A checks and balances between the Requiring Activity and Contracting. They request the funds (commit) from the Finance Operations Section. When the Contracting Officer signs the Contract. The Resource Manager will obligate the funds. They cannot obligate the funds without the Contracting Officers Signature on a contract.

Legal – An attorney or attorneys that are designated to review the acquisition package, fiscal law, Appropriations Act, and Authorization Act. Their focus is to cover the Government from violations of a finance violation, due to the color of money not being like the Commercial Sector. Money is money in the Commercial sector, but in the Government certain dollars can only be paid to certain items. This is known as color of money.

Legal review is an important component of any requirements/acquisition package that the requiring activity provided, but to look over the Contracting/Acquisition Management solicitation that was put together with the requiring activities documentation. They mitigate the risk and try to reduce any ambiguities that may arise.

Contracting/Acquisition Management – provides the full range of professional procurement and grant services to customers worldwide, including acquisition planning, contract negotiations, cost and price analysis, and contract administration. The two main employees in Acquisition Management are the following:

- Contracting Officer Representative (COR) – eyes and years of the Contracting Officer. They assist the Contracting officer in technical monitoring or administration of the contract. The Contracting Officer appoints the COR to the Contract.

- Contract Specialist – creates, examines and monitors contractual agreements between the organization that he or she works for and materials or labor supplier.

- Contracting Officer – have authority to enter into, administer, or terminate contracts and make related determinations and findings. Contracting officers may bind the Government only to the extent of the authority delegated to them. Contracting officers shall receive from the appointing authority; clear instructions in writing regarding the limits of their authority. Information on the limits of the contracting officers' authority shall be readily available to the public and agency personnel.

No contract shall be entered into unless the Contracting Officer ensures that all requirements of law, executive orders, regulations, and all other applicable procedures,   including clearances and approvals, have been met.

LAW: 48 CFR 1352.201-70 - Contracting Officer's Authority.

The Contracting Officer is the only person authorized to make or approve any changes in any of the requirements of this contract, and, notwithstanding any provisions contained elsewhere in this contract, the said authority remains solely in the Contracting Officer. In the event the contractor makes any changes at the direction of any person other than the Contracting

Officer, the change will be considered to have been made without authority and no adjustment will be made in the contract terms and conditions, including price.

IAW FAR Subpart 1.602-2(d)(5)

The Contracting Officer's Representative (COR) has no authority to make any commitments or changes that affect price, quality, quantity, delivery, or other terms and conditions of the contract nor in any way direct the contractor or its subcontractors to operate in conflict with the contract terms and conditions;

𝔓𝔯𝔬𝔠𝔢𝔰𝔰 𝔅𝔢𝔩𝔬𝔴 𝔖𝔦𝔪𝔭𝔩𝔦𝔣𝔦𝔢𝔡 𝔄𝔠𝔮𝔲𝔦𝔰𝔦𝔱𝔦𝔬𝔫𝔰 $250,000

1. Requiring Activity – determines what needs to be procured.

2. Resource Manager – requests the funds from the Finance Operations.

3. Finance Operations – accounts for the funding that the resource manager has requested.

4. Resource Manager – is notified by the finance office if the funds are available. If funds are available, the packet moves forward. If not, the requirement is known as "subject to availability of funds" and can still move forward.

5. Requiring Activity – Once funds are known or not known the packet is sent up for approvals and routed to the Contracting/Acquisition Management Office.

6. Contracting/Acquisition Management – will review the requirements/acquisitions package for completeness. If not complete or discrepancies the package is sent back to the requiring activity to fix.

7. Requiring Activity – fix errors if any.

8. Contracting/Acquisitions Management – reviews the package and develops supporting documents from market research to determination & findings. Finally, the solicitation to be solicited.

9. Solicitations are posted – can be posted on www.gsaadvantage.gov or FedBid now known as Unison Marketplace – reverse auction https://www.unisonglobal.com/product-suites/acquisition/sourcing/marketplace/ or www.fbo.gov

10. Contracting/Acquisitions Management – request for information may be received and sent to the requiring activity to answer. Updates to the solicitation through amendments and collecting of the quotes, bids, or proposals occur. Once all the quotes, bids, or proposals are received the Contract Specialist or Contracting Officer will do a review of the quotes, or proposals for completeness. Check www.sam.gov plus past performance in CPARS or FAPIIS and to determine if the vendor/contractor is responsive.

11. Requiring Activity – The responsive vendors/contractors are sent to the requiring activity to do a technical review IAW the evaluation factors and make a decision on who the awarded vendor/contractor will be. The vendor is considered technically acceptable.

12. Contracting/Acquisitions Management – receives the technical evaluation, determines fair and reasonable, & determination of responsibility. If the funding is already there, then writes the contract & distributes the contract to all parties (resource manager, finance, requiring activity, and vendor/business). Which will obligate the funds, but the Resource Manager confirms the obligation of funds once the Contract is received.

- If funding is not available, it is requested from the requiring activity, to the resource manager, finance operations and back down to award the contract.

13. The contractor/vendor also known as the awardee is notified. The remaining vendors should be notified that the contract was awarded.

𝔓𝔯𝔬𝔠𝔢𝔰𝔰 𝔄𝔟𝔬𝔳𝔢 𝔖𝔦𝔪𝔭𝔩𝔦𝔣𝔦𝔢𝔡 𝔄𝔠𝔮𝔲𝔦𝔰𝔦𝔱𝔦𝔬𝔫𝔰 $250,000

1. Requiring Activity – determines what needs to be procured. This is usually 18 months out or longer, but can be sooner as well. This is where a Procurement Development Team (PDT) is determined that consists of the requiring activity, technical personal, and contracting. The acquisition/requirements package should be developed as a team for a smooth transition to be procured.

   a. Note: This does not always occur.

2. Resource Manager – requests the funds from the Finance Operations.

3. Finance Operations – accounts for the funding that the resource manager has requested.

4. Resource Manager – is notified by the finance office if the funds are available. If funds are available, the packet moves forward. If not, the requirement is known as "subject to availability of funds" and can still move forward.

5. Requiring Activity – Once funds are known or not known the packet is sent up for approvals and routed to the Contracting/Acquisition Management Office.

6. Contracting/Acquisition Management – will review the requirement/acquisition package for completeness. If not complete or discrepancies the package is sent back to the

requiring activity to fix. Yes, there was the PDT, but that doesn't always resolve everything. If the package is complete then documentation is filled out, solicitation completed, then sent for reviews and signatures for approval. This is known as the solicitation review board.

7. Legal – Reviews the requirements/acquisition package in the same manner as the reviews. Legal is a part of the solicitation review board.

8. Contracting/Acquisitions Management – once the reviews are completed, contracting will post a synopsis stating that this requirement is coming (sometimes concurrent with the review process).

9. Solicitation is posted.

10. Contracting/Acquisitions Management – receives all the quotes or proposals.

11. Source Selection – process of evaluating a competitive bid or proposal to enter into a Government procurement contract. The term "source selection" is used for referring to acquisitions awarded according to Federal Acquisition Regulation Parts 13 (Simplified Acquisition), 14 (Sealed Bidding), or 15 (Contracting by Negotiation). The source selection usually consists of contracting, the requiring activity who provides the technical experts.

12. Contracting/Acquisitions Management – decision is made, and a contract review board is conducted. This review board is the same process as the solicitation review board with the reviews and signatures for approval.

    a. Depending on the agency the determination of fair and reasonable and determination of responsibility

13. Legal – Reviews the requirements/acquisition package in the same manner as the reviews. Legal is a part of the contract review board.

14. Contracting/Acquisitions Management –. If the funding is already available, distributes the contract to all parties (resource manager, finance, requiring activity, and vendor/business). Which will obligate the funds.

    a. If funding is not available, it is requested from the requiring activity, to the resource manager, finance operations and back down to award the contract.

15. The Resource Manager confirms the obligation of funds once the Contract is received.

16. The contractor/vendor also known as the awardee is notified. The remaining vendors should be notified that the contract was awarded.

17. The notice is posted on www.fbo.gov

Note: *The acquisition process varies by Government Agency. There may be more steps/approval processes or even documents. Each agency is different. This is a general process to be followed.*

✓ **Calling the Government, asking them to buy your product or service.**

✓ **The Requiring Activity determines the need. Not the Contracting Officer.**

✓ **There is an approval process.**

✓ **There is a reason why the Requiring Activity Point of Contact(s) are not known.**

✓ **The separation of powers/fiscal triad exist to mitigate back room deals and ethical violations.**

Chapter 2 - Market Research

The Requiring Activity can be anyone within the Government that defines the need. Majority of the time it is a program office or individuals within a program office such as logistics, information technology, or facilities. That requiring activity can be someone in Management as well. Before they present what the "need" is, they shall develop what the need is and how much it will cost. This is completed through market research.

Market Research is in accordance with the Federal Acquisition Regulation - Part 10; which states, "*This part prescribes policies and procedures for conducting market research to arrive at the most suitable approach to acquiring, distributing, and supporting supplies and services.*"

Procedures

Acquisitions begin with a description of the Government's needs stated in terms sufficient to allow conduct of market research. Market research is then conducted to determine if commercial items or nondevelopmental items are available to meet the Government's needs or could be modified to meet the Government's needs.

Commercial Item means --

(1) Any item, other than real property, that is of a type customarily used by the general public or by non-Governmental entities for purposes other than Governmental purposes, and--

(i) Has been sold, leased, or licensed to the general public; or,

(ii) Has been offered for sale, lease, or license to the general public;

(2) Any item that evolved from an item described in paragraph (1) of this definition through advances in technology or performance and that is not yet available in the commercial marketplace, but will be available in the commercial marketplace in time to satisfy the delivery requirements under a Government solicitation;

(3) Any item that would satisfy a criterion expressed in paragraphs (1) or (2) of this definition, but for --

    (i) Modifications of a type customarily available in the commercial marketplace; or

    (ii) Minor modifications of a type not customarily available in the commercial marketplace made to meet Federal Government requirements. Minor modifications means modifications that do not significantly alter the Non-Governmental function or essential physical characteristics of an item or component, or change the purpose of a process. Factors to be considered in determining whether a modification is minor include the value and size of the modification and the comparative value and size of the final product. Dollar values and percentages may be used as guideposts, but are not conclusive evidence that a modification is minor;

(4) Any combination of items meeting the requirements of paragraphs (1), (2), (3), or (5) of this definition that are of a type customarily combined and sold in combination to the general public;

(5) Installation services, maintenance services, repair services, training services, and other services if--

    (i) Such services are procured for support of an item referred to in paragraph (1), (2), (3), or (4) of this definition, regardless of whether such services are provided by the same source or at the same time as the item; and

    (ii) The source of such services provides similar services contemporaneously to the general public under terms and conditions similar to those offered to the Federal Government;

(6) Services of a type offered and sold competitively in substantial quantities in the commercial marketplace based on established catalog or market prices for specific tasks performed or specific outcomes to be achieved and under standard commercial terms and conditions. For purposes of these services—

    (i) "Catalog price" means a price included in a catalog, price list, schedule, or other form that is regularly maintained by the manufacturer or vendor, is either published or otherwise available for inspection by customers, and states prices at which sales are currently, or were last, made to a significant number of buyers constituting the general public; and

    (ii) "Market prices" means current prices that are established in the course of ordinary trade between buyers and sellers free to bargain and that can be substantiated through competition or from sources independent of the offerors.

(7) Any item, combination of items, or service referred to in paragraphs (1) through (6) of this definition, notwithstanding the fact that the item, combination of items, or service is transferred between or among separate divisions, subsidiaries, or affiliates of a contractor; or

(8) A **nondevelopmental item**, if the procuring agency determines the item was developed exclusively at private expense and sold in substantial quantities, on a competitive basis, to multiple State and local Governments.

(1) The extent of market research will vary, depending on such factors as urgency, estimated dollar value, complexity, and past experience. The contracting officer may use market research conducted within 18 months before the award of any task or delivery order if the information is still current, accurate, and relevant. Market

research involves obtaining information specific to the item being acquired and should include

(i) Whether the Government's needs can be met by --

(A) Items of a type customarily available in the commercial marketplace;

(B) Items of a type customarily available in the commercial marketplace with modifications; or

(C) Items used exclusively for Governmental purposes;

(ii) Customary practices regarding customizing, modifying or tailoring of items to meet customer needs and associated costs;

(iii) Customary practices, including warranty, buyer financing, discounts, contract type considering the nature and risk associated with the requirement, etc., under which commercial sales of the products are made;

(iv) The requirements of any laws and regulations unique to the item being acquired;

(v) The availability of items that contain recovered materials and items that are energy efficient;

(vi) The distribution and support capabilities of potential suppliers, including alternative arrangements and cost estimates; and

(vii) Size and status of potential sources.

(2) Techniques for conducting market research may include any or all of the following:

(i) Contacting knowledgeable individuals in Government and industry regarding market capabilities to meet requirements.

(ii) Reviewing the results of recent market research undertaken to meet similar or identical requirements.

(iii) Publishing formal requests for information in appropriate technical or scientific journals or business publications.

(iv) Querying the Governmentwide database of contracts and other procurement instruments intended for use by multiple agencies available at https://www.contractdirectory.gov/contractdirectory/ and other Government and commercial databases that provide information relevant to agency acquisitions.

(v) Participating in interactive, on-line communication among industry, acquisition personnel, and customers.

(vi) Obtaining source lists of similar items from other contracting activities or agencies, trade associations or other sources.

(vii) Reviewing catalogs and other generally available product literature published by manufacturers, distributors, and dealers or available on-line.

(viii) Conducting interchange meetings or holding presolicitation conferences to involve potential offerors early in the acquisition process.

Policy

(a) Agencies shall --

   (1) Ensure that legitimate needs are identified, and trade-offs evaluated to acquire items that meet those needs;

   (2) Conduct market research appropriate to the circumstances --

       (i) Before developing new requirements documents for an acquisition by that agency;

       (ii) Before soliciting offers for acquisitions with an estimated value more than the simplified acquisition threshold ($250,000);

       (iii) Before soliciting offers for acquisitions with an estimated value less than the simplified acquisition threshold when adequate information is not available, and the circumstances justify its cost;

       (iv) Before soliciting offers for acquisitions that could lead to

           • Consolidation or consolidated requirement

               (1) Means a solicitation for a single contract, a multiple-award contract, a task order, or a delivery order to satisfy--

                   (i) Two or more requirements of the Federal agency for supplies or services that have been provided to or performed for the Federal agency under two or more separate contracts, each of which was lower in cost than the total cost of the contract for which offers are solicited; or

(ii) Requirements of the Federal agency for construction projects to be performed at two or more discrete sites.

(2) Separate contract as used in this definition, means a contract that has been performed by any business, including small and other than small business concerns.

- Bundling

(1) Means a subset of consolidation that combines two or more requirements for supplies or services, previously provided or performed under separate smaller contracts (see paragraph (2) of this definition), into a solicitation for a single contract, a multiple-award contract, or a task or delivery order that is likely to be unsuitable for award to a small business concern (even if it is suitable for award to a small business with a Small Business Teaming Arrangement) due to--

(i) The diversity, size, or specialized nature of the elements of the performance specified;

(ii) The aggregate dollar value of the anticipated award;

(iii) The geographical dispersion of the contract performance sites; or

(iv) Any combination of the factors described in paragraphs (1)(i), (ii), and (iii) of this definition.

(2) "Separate smaller contract" as used in this definition, means a contract that has been performed by one or more small business concerns or that was suitable for award to one or more small business concerns.

(3) This definition does not apply to a contract that will be awarded and performed entirely outside of the United States.

(v) Before awarding a task or delivery order under an indefinite-delivery-indefinite-quantity (ID/IQ) contract (*e.g.*, GWACs, MACs) for a noncommercial item in excess of the simplified acquisition threshold; and

(vi) On an ongoing basis, take advantage (to the maximum extent practicable) of commercially available market research methods in order to effectively identify the capabilities of small businesses and new entrants into Federal contracting, that are available in the marketplace for meeting the requirements of the agency in furtherance of—

(A) A contingency operation or defense against or recovery from nuclear, biological, chemical or radiological attack; and

(B) Disaster relief to include debris removal, distribution of supplies, reconstruction, and other disaster or emergency relief activities.

(3) Use the results of market research to --

(i) Determine if sources capable of satisfying the agency's requirements exist;

(ii) Determine if commercial items or, to the extent commercial items suitable to meet the agency's needs are not available, nondevelopmental items are available that --

    (A) Meet the agency's requirements;

    (B) Could be modified to meet the agency's requirements; or

    (C) Could meet the agency's requirements if those requirements were modified to a reasonable extent;

(iii) Determine the extent to which commercial items or nondevelopmental items could be incorporated at the component level;

(iv) Determine the practices of firms engaged in producing, distributing, and supporting commercial items, such as type of contract, terms for warranties, buyer financing, maintenance and packaging, and marking;

(v) Ensure maximum practicable use of recovered materials and promote energy conservation and efficiency;

(vi) Determine whether consolidation is necessary and justified.

(vii) Determine whether bundling is necessary and justified.

(viii) Assess the availability of electronic and information technology that meets all or part of the applicability standards issued by the Architectural and Transportation Barriers Compliance Board at 36 CFR part 1194.

(b) When conducting market research, agencies should not request potential sources to submit more than the minimum information necessary.

(c) If an agency contemplates consolidation or bundling, the agency —

(1) When performing market research, should consult with the agency small business specialist and the local Small Business Administration procurement center representative (PCR). If a PCR is not assigned, review the following site to find a representative to support the market research https://www.sba.gov/partners/contracting-officials/contract-administration

(2) Shall notify any affected incumbent small business concerns of the Government's intention to bundle the requirement and how small business concerns may contact the appropriate Small Business Administration procurement center representative.

Reference: http://farsite.hill.af.mil/vmfara.htm or https://acquisition.gov/browse/index/far

Vendor Searches

The Government will search for vendors to determine if there are vendors capable of performing the requirement that the Government needs accomplished through the procedures outlined in this chapter. Four tools that Contract Specialist and Contracting Officers conduct searches are through these four methods:

1. Sources Sought – is not an actual bid or proposal solicitation; instead, it's a solicitation of interest. Think of a Sources Sought as market research being conducted by a government

agency to determine what the capabilities and interests of the marketplace are. Look at www.fbo.gov

2. Historical Contract – www.usaspending.gov

3. System for Award Management – www.sam.gov

4. Small Business Administration - Dynamic Small Business Search -

    http://dsbs.sba.gov/dsbs/search/dsp_dsbs.cfm

1. Sources Sought

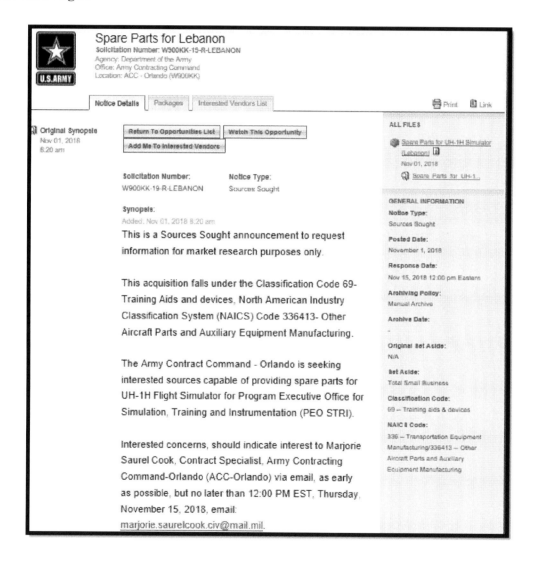

Spare Parts for Lebanon
Solicitation Number: W900KK-19-R-LEBANON
Agency: Department of the Army
Office: Army Contracting Command
Location: ACC - Orlando (W900KK)

Notice Details | Packages | Interested Vendors List

🖶 Print   📖 Link

Original Synopsis
Nov 01, 2018
8:20 am

Return To Opportunities List   Watch This Opportunity

Add Me To Interested Vendors

Solicitation Number: **Notice Type:**
W900KK-19-R-LEBANON   Sources Sought

Synopsis:
Added: Nov 01, 2018 8:20 am

This is a Sources Sought announcement to request information for market research purposes only.

This acquisition falls under the Classification Code 69-Training Aids and devices, North American Industry Classification System (NAICS) Code 336413- Other Aircraft Parts and Auxiliary Equipment Manufacturing.

The Army Contract Command - Orlando is seeking interested sources capable of providing spare parts for UH-1H Flight Simulator for Program Executive Office for Simulation, Training and Instrumentation (PEO STRI).

Interested concerns, should indicate interest to Marjorie Saurel Cook, Contract Specialist, Army Contracting Command-Orlando (ACC-Orlando) via email, as early as possible, but no later than 12:00 PM EST, Thursday, November 15, 2018, email: marjorie.saurelcook.civ@mail.mil.

ALL FILES

📎 Spare Parts for UH-1H Simulator (Lebanon) 📄
Nov 01, 2018
📄 Spare Parts for UH-1...

GENERAL INFORMATION
Notice Type:
Sources Sought

Posted Date:
November 1, 2018

Response Date:
Nov 15, 2018 12:00 pm Eastern

Archiving Policy:
Manual Archive

Archive Date:
-

Original Set Aside:
N/A

Set Aside:
Total Small Business

Classification Code:
69 -- Training aids & devices

NAICS Code:
336 -- Transportation Equipment Manufacturing/336413 -- Other Aircraft Parts and Auxiliary Equipment Manufacturing

Please consult the list of document viewers if you cannot open a file.

 Spare Parts for UH-1H Simulator (Lebanon)

Type: Other (Draft RFPs/RFIs, Responses to Questions, etc..)

Posted Date: November 1, 2018

Spare_Parts_for_UH-1H_simulator.pdf (1,289.72 Kb)

Description: Spare Parts for UH-1H Simulator

Contracting Office Address:

12211 Science Drive

Orlando, Florida 32826-3224

United States

Place of Performance:

Lebanon

United States

Primary Point of Contact.:

Marjorie Saurel Cook,

Contract Specialist

marjorie.saurelcook.civ@mail.mil

Phone: 4072083398

Return To Opportunities List	Watch This Opportunity
Add Me To Interested Vendors	

2. Historical Contracts – www.usaspending.gov

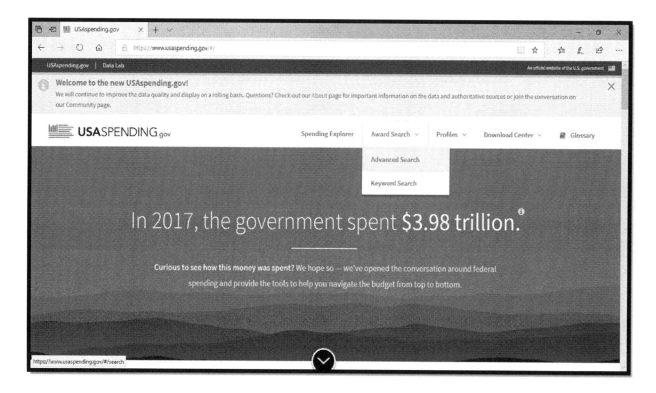

Step 1:

1. https://www.usaspending.gov

2. Put curser also known as mouse arrow over award search

3. Select advance searched (click)

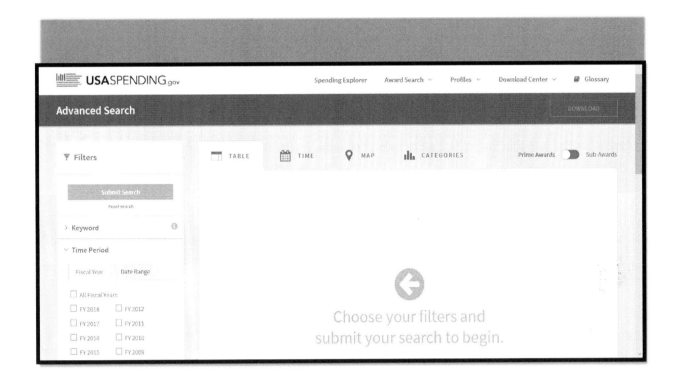

Step 2:

1. IAW to FAR Subpart 10.002(b)(1) the extent of market research will vary, depending on such factors as urgency, estimated dollar value, complexity, and past experience. The contracting officer may use market research conducted within 18 months before the award of any task or delivery order if the information is still current, accurate, and relevant.

2. Tap Date Range

Step 3:

1. Enter – 18 months from today.

2. Leave End Date Blank

3. Tape the magnifying class

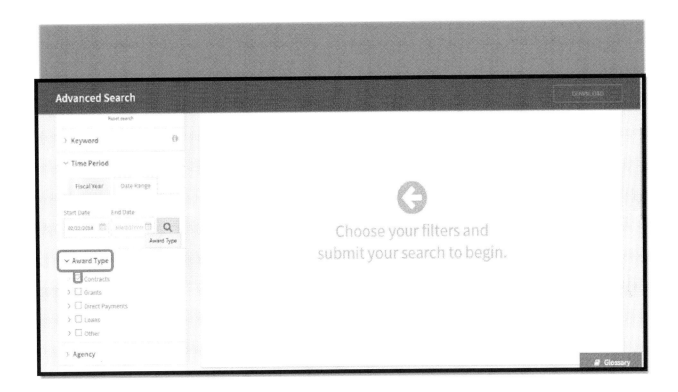

Step 4:

1. Tap the Award Type drop down menu.

2. Put a check into the Contracts box.

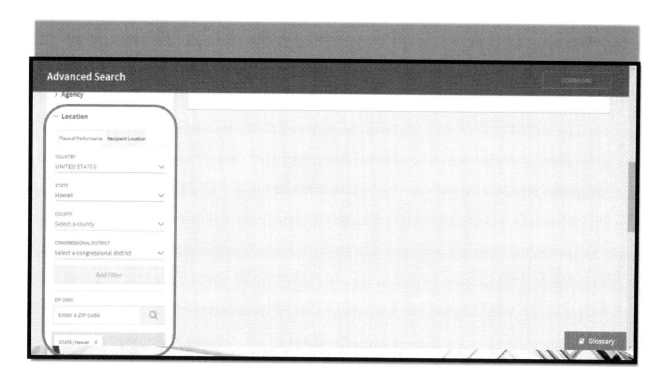

Step 5:

1. Scroll down to location – press tab.

2. Country – United States

3. State – Hawaii

4. Tap add Filter

Step 6:

1. Scroll Down and tap NAICS Code

2. Put in NAICS Code 561612

3. It will highlight the box, click the box and it will populate.

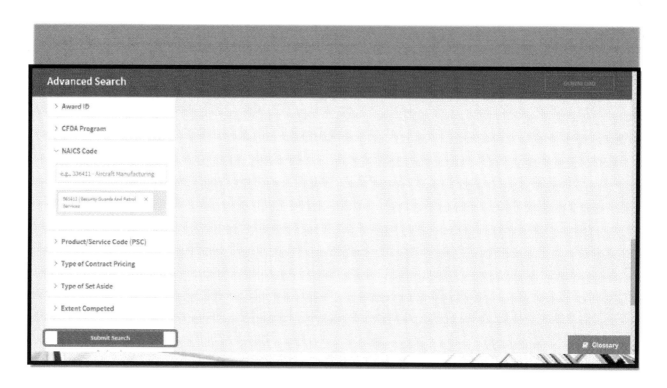

Step 7:

    1. Hit Submit Search

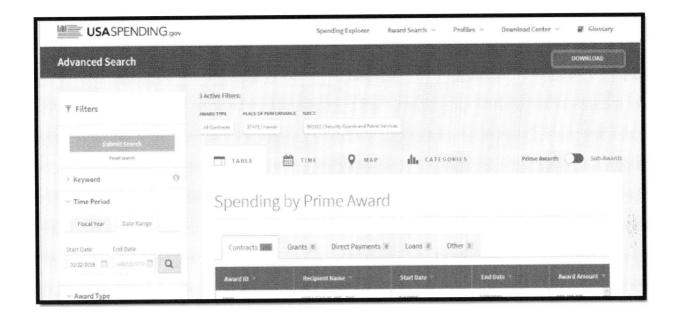

Step 8:

1. Scroll back to the top.

2. Hit the blue button that has "Download"

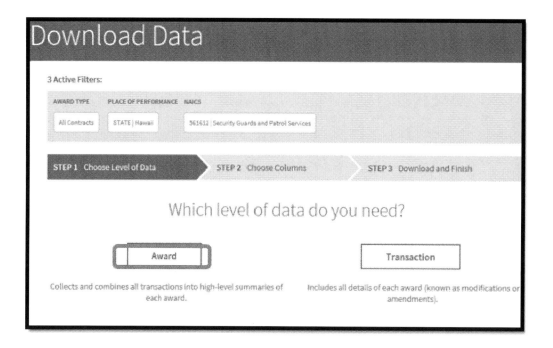

Step 9:

1. Tap the award with your mouse

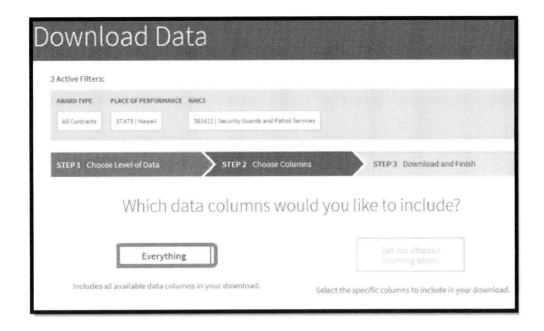

Step 10:

1. Tap the Everything with your mouse

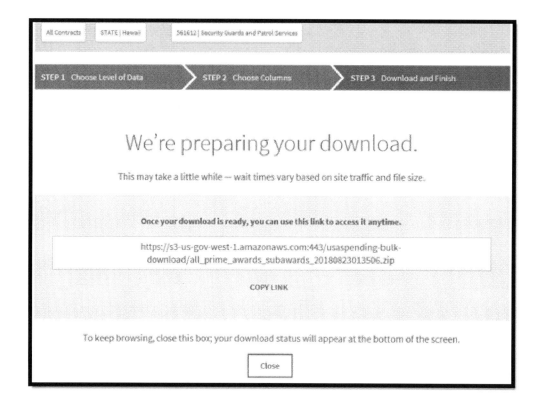

Step 11:

1. Wait, wait, wait

2. Open the folder and save the prime document as an excel. The document will attempt to save as a CVS.

Name	Size	Packed Size
all_assistance_prime_aw...	1 655	430
all_assistance_subaward...	984 233	154 007
all_contracts_prime_aw...		14 087
all_contracts_subawards...		80 490

Step 12:

1. Open and Save As All_Contracts_prime_award as an excel

3. System for Award Management – www.sam.gov

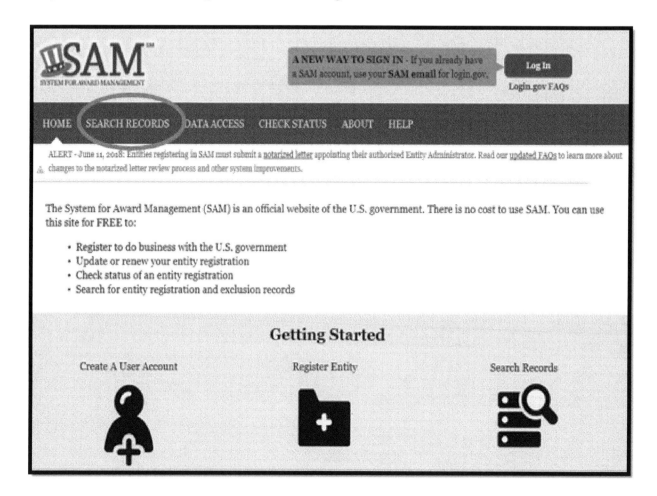

Step 1:

1. Tap on Search Records

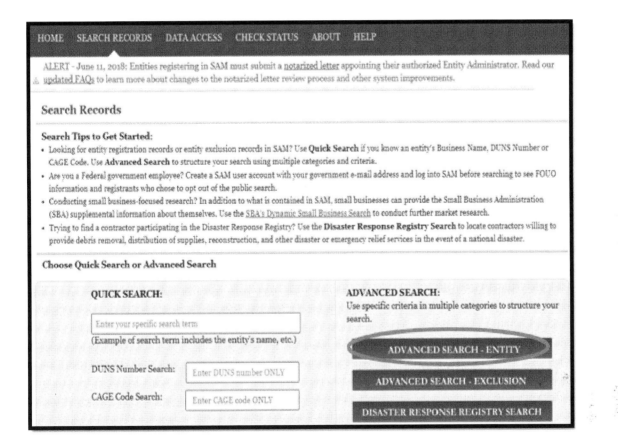

Step 2:

1. Click on Advanced Search - Entity

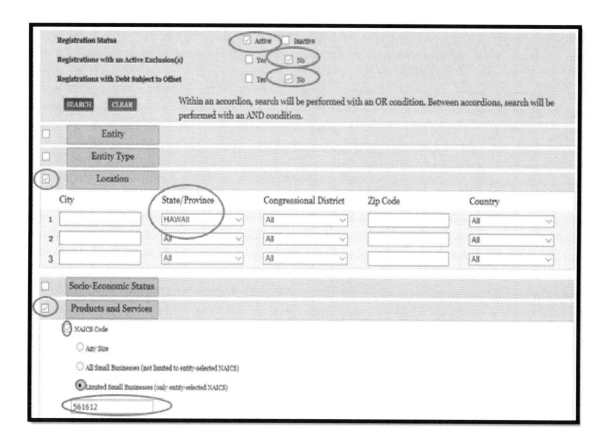

Step 3:

1. Registration Status – Check Active
2. Registrations with an Active Exclusion(s) – Check No
3. Registrations with Debt Subject to Offset – Check No
4. Check box in Location
5. State/Province – put in state (Hawaii is used)
6. Check product and services
7. Check NAICS Codes

8. Fill in bubble Limited Small Business (Only entity-select NAICS)
9. Type in NAICS code – 561612 is used (Security Guards and Patrol Services)

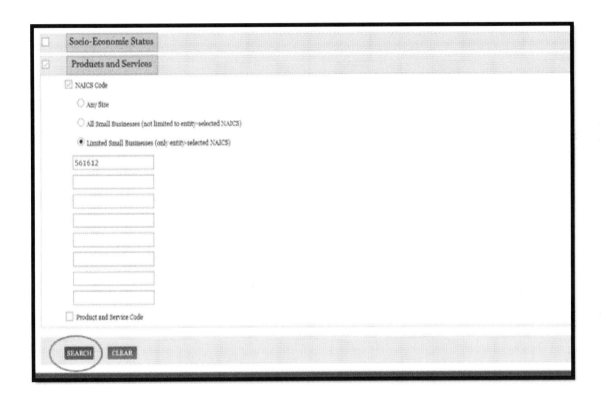

Step 4:
    1. Scroll Down and hit Search

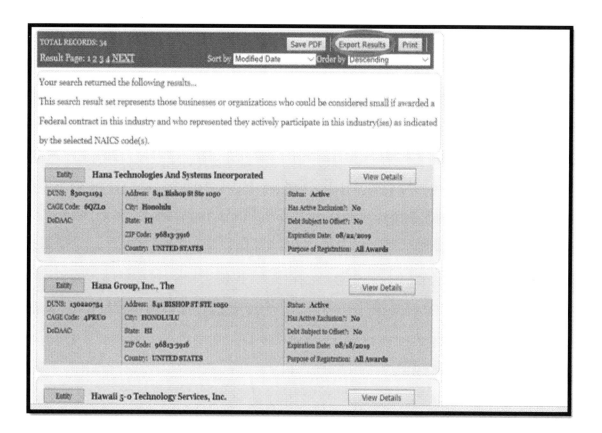

Step 5:

1. Scroll Up

2. Hit Export Results

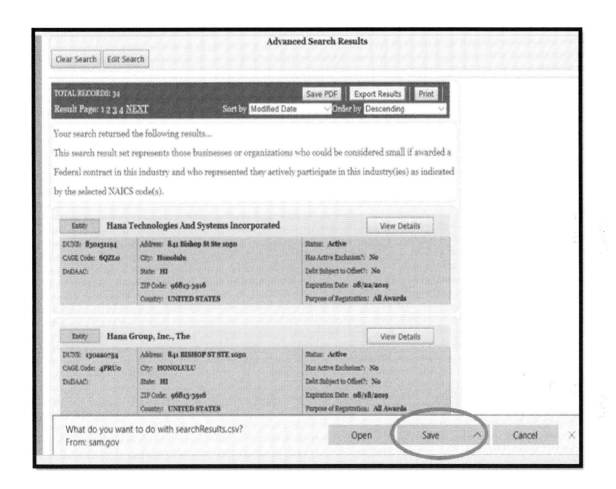

Step 6:

1. Hit Save

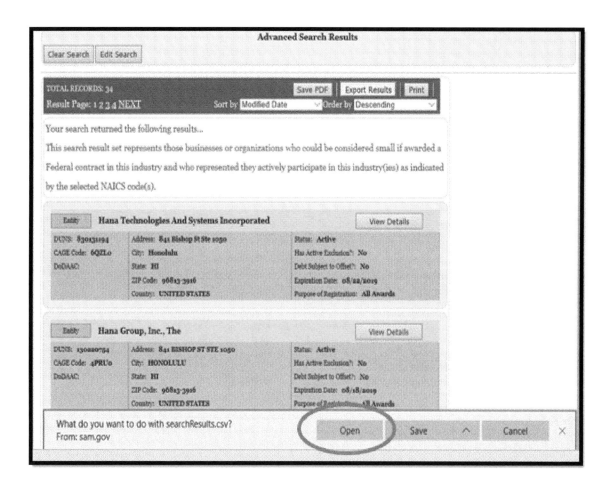

Step 7:

1. Then Hit Open

2. Make sure you Save As

3. Make sure it is an excel document

4. Small Business Administration - Dynamic Small Business Search

Link - http://dsbs.sba.gov/dsbs/search/dsp_dsbs.cfm

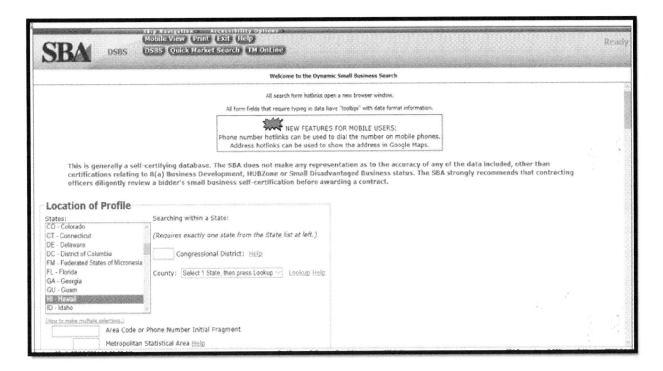

Step 1:

1. Scroll down to Location of Profile

2. Select State

3. To select multiple States, hold CTL and select

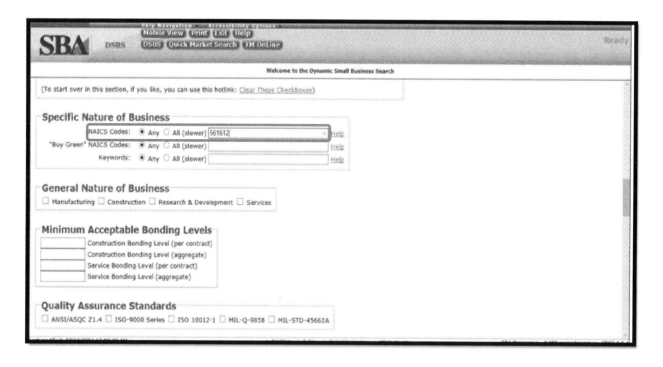

Step 2:

1. Scroll down to NAICS Code and type in the NAICS

2. 561612

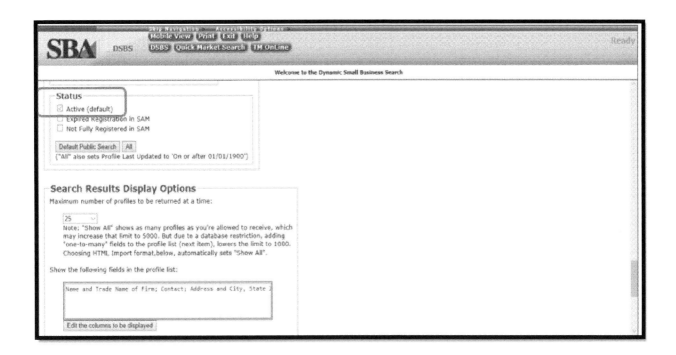

Step 3:

1. Scroll down to Status

2. Check Active (default)

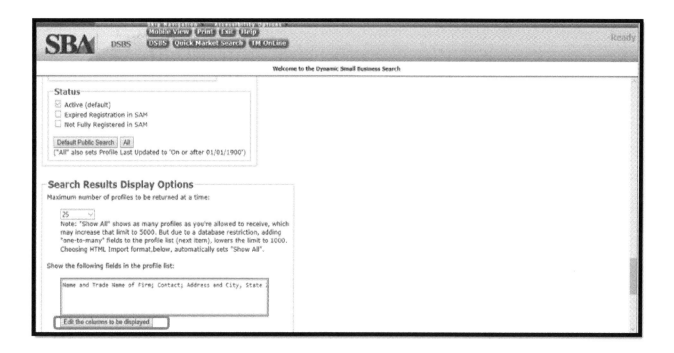

Step 4:

1. Tap Edit the Columns to be displayed

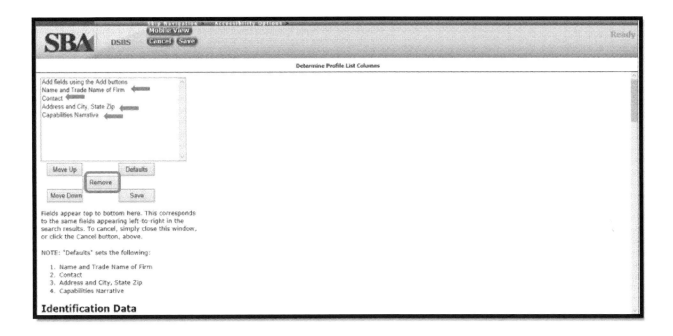

Step 5:

1. A Window will pop open

2. Select – Name and Trade Name of Firms – then tap remove

3. Select – Contact – then tap remove

4. Select – Address and City, State Zip – then tap remove

5. Select – Capabilities Narrative – then tap remove

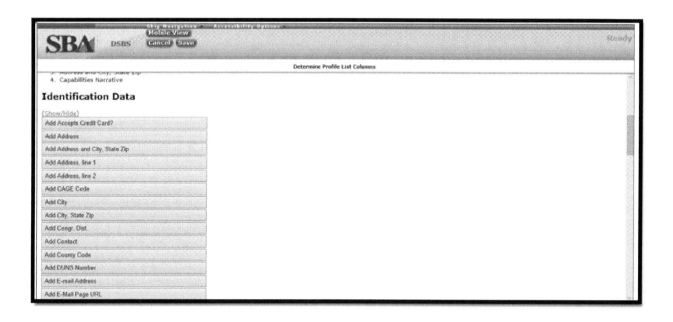

Step 6:

1. Scroll Down and tap on the following in this order (12 total)
2. Add Name of Firm
3. Add Duns Number
4. Add Address
5. Add City
6. Add County Code
7. Add State
8. Add Zip
9. Add Contact
10. Add Phone Number
11. Add Fax Number
12. Add E-mail address
13. Add E-mail Page URL

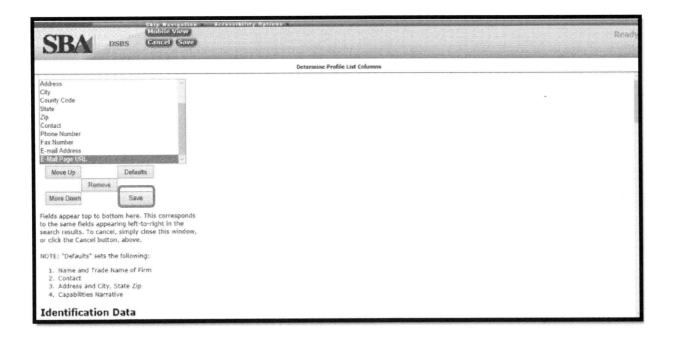

Step 7:

1. Scroll back up

2. Hit Save – make sure you hit save

3. Window will go away.

Step 8:

1. Scroll down

2. Tap radial button for HTML Import Format

3. Tap radial button for xls (Spreadsheet)

4. Tap Search Using These Criteria

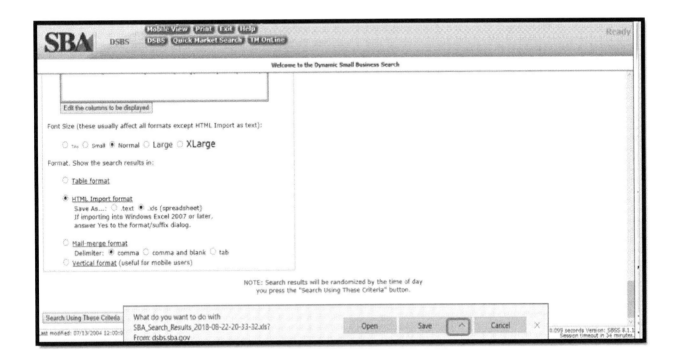

Step 9:

1. Tap arrow

2. Tap save as

Chapter 3 – Back Room Deals

Back Room Deals are Illegal!!

Contractors in my experience as a Contract Specialist and Contracting Officer working

for the U.S. Army Mission Installation Contracting Command, Federal Emergency Management

Agency, and U.S. Army Corps of Engineers would send in gifts, try to become friendly and the

daily capabilities statement. According to Chapter 1 - Separation of Powers/Positions – The

Fiscal Triad, you as a contractor/business owner now know that Government Sales is not like the following sales:

- Business to consumer, (B2C), refers to the transactions conducted directly between a company and consumers who are the end-users of its products or services. The business to consumer as a business model differs significantly from the business-to-business model, which refers to commerce between two or more businesses.

- Business to business, (B2B), is a form of transaction between businesses, such as one involving a manufacturer and wholesaler, or a wholesaler and a retailer. Business to business refers to business that is conducted between companies, rather than between a company and individual consumers.

I have been in meetings where I hear million-dollar companies state, "*that they only want to compete on contracts that are above $1,000,000 plus.*" If the company does not have the past performance may be an evaluation factor. If the resulting contract is over $250,000. It is an evaluation factor. The Government may not accept commercial work as a past performance and only Government. It depends on how the past performance is being evaluated. See the reasons why:

1. <u>FAR Subpart 15.101 -- Best Value Continuum</u>. An agency can obtain best value in negotiated acquisitions by using any one or a combination of source selection approaches. In different types of acquisitions, the relative importance of cost or price may vary. For example, in acquisitions where the requirement is clearly definable, and the risk of unsuccessful contract performance is minimal, cost or price may play a dominant role in source selection. The less definitive the requirement, the more development work required, or the greater the performance risk, the more technical *or past performance considerations may play a dominant role in source selection.*

2. <u>FAR Subpart 15.101-2 -- Lowest Price Technically Acceptable Source Selection Process</u>. The evaluation factors and significant subfactors that establish the requirements of acceptability shall be set forth in the solicitation. Solicitations shall specify that award will be made on the basis of the lowest evaluated price of proposals meeting or exceeding the acceptability standards for non-cost factors. If the contracting officer documents the file pursuant to:

   - FAR Subpart 15.304(c)(3)(iii), *past performance need not be an evaluation factor* in lowest price technically acceptable source selections. If the contracting officer elects to <u>consider past performance as an evaluation factor</u>, it shall be evaluated in accordance with 15.305 Proposal Evaluation.

- o Past performance evaluation.

    (i) Past performance information is one indicator of an offeror's ability to perform the contract successfully. The currency and relevance of the information, source of the information, context of the data, and general trends in contractor's performance shall be considered. This comparative assessment of past performance information is separate from the responsibility determination.

    (ii) The solicitation shall describe the approach for evaluating past performance, including evaluating offerors with no relevant performance history, and shall provide offerors an opportunity to identify past or current contracts (including Federal, State, and local government and private) for efforts similar to the Government requirement. The solicitation shall also authorize offerors to provide information on problems encountered on the identified contracts and the offeror corrective actions. The Government shall consider this information, as well as information obtained from any other sources, when evaluating the offeror past performance. The source selection authority shall determine the relevance of similar past performance information.

(iii) The evaluation should take into account past performance information regarding predecessor companies, key personnel who have relevant experience, or subcontractors that will perform major or critical aspects of the requirement when such information is relevant to the instant acquisition.

(iv) In the case of an offeror without a record of relevant past performance or for whom information on past performance is not available, the offeror may not be evaluated favorably or unfavorably on past performance.

(v) The evaluation should include the past performance of offerors in complying with subcontracting plan goals for small disadvantaged business (SDB) concerns.

- However, the comparative assessment in 15.305(a)(2)(i) does not apply. Past performance information is one indicator of an offeror's ability to perform the contract successfully. The currency and relevance of the information, source of the information, context of the data, and general trends in contractor's performance shall be considered. This comparative assessment of past performance information is separate from the responsibility determination.

- If the contracting officer determines that a small business' past performance is not acceptable, the matter shall be referred to the Small Business Administration for a Certificate of Competency determination.

Other lines that I hear are:

1. *"I know this General and he/she said I could have a Government contract."*

2. *"I know this Senator and he/she said I could have a Government Contract."*

3. *"(Insert name) (title) said, "I will be awarded this Contract."*

4. *"Do you know who I am?"*

5. *"If I do not get this contract, I will sue you personally."*

Reminder IAW to LAW: 48 CFR 1352.201-70 - Contracting Officer's Authority.

The Contracting Officer is the only person authorized to make or approve any changes in any of the requirements of this contract, and, notwithstanding any provisions contained elsewhere in this contract, the said authority remains solely in the Contracting Officer. In the event the contractor makes any changes at the direction of any person other than the Contracting Officer, the change will be considered to have been made without authority and no adjustment will be made in the contract terms and conditions, including price.

Legal Cases

Government Employees

Chris Isidore of CNN Money published on February 12, 2017, <u>Here's what happens when you violate Government Ethics Rules</u> that in 2015 that 1,584 violation rules. The most common violation were offenses such as promoting a product or service that would be beneficial to a federal employee, their friends or family members.

- An Army Lieutenant Colonel was sentenced to three years in prison for accepting a $253,000 payment from two Army Contractors in exchange for favoring the companies in the bidding process for work with the Army.

- An employee with the General Services Administration responsible for overseeing two ports of entry was sentenced to 16 months in prison and required to pay $50,000 for demanding bribes from contractors.

- A financial administrator for the Federal Bureau of Prison was given three years' probation and paid a $5,000 fine for failing to disclose a business relationship he had with a Federal Contractor that was competing to provide inmate health care services.

Reference: https://money.cnn.com/2017/02/12/news/ethical-violation-penalties/

Contractors/Vendors/Business have also been penalized for violating ethics.

The Project on Government Oversight was founded in 1981 and their mission is nonpartisan independent watchdog that champions good government reforms. POGO's investigations into corruption, misconduct, and conflicts of interest achieve a more effective, accountable, open, and ethical federal government. Their database allows anyone to search for misconduct and alleged misconduct.

Reference: https://www.contractormisconduct.org/about-fcmd

1. MCC Construction Company (MCC) has agreed to pay $1,769,294 in criminal penalties and forfeiture for conspiring to commit fraud on the United States by illegally obtaining government contracts that were intended for small, disadvantaged businesses. "MCC Construction Company secured millions of dollars in contracts by hiding behind two small businesses that did not perform labor on the projects. Its conduct took away opportunities that could have gone to companies that truly are socially and economically disadvantaged and deserving of the work." An uneven marketplace is created when businesses engage in illegal backroom deals to fraudulently obtain government contracts, placing competitors at an unfair disadvantage.

2. In 2012, the state hired a private vendor to help rein in out-of-control costs associated with Illinois' nearly $20 billion Medicaid program. Republican state Sens. Dale Righter and Patti Bellock accused the Quinn administration of cutting a "backroom deal" with the largest state employee union that will dismantle efforts to crack down on Medicaid fraud.

By outsourcing the oversight of Medicaid program to a contractor; which allowed for an eligibility error rate of more than 60 percent for individuals that applied.

Penalties for backroom deals can lead to prison time, fines, and debarment from pursuing Government Contracts.

Chapter 4 - Ethics violations

Chapter 4 describes ethical violations that occur and the penalties that shall occur if convicted. This chapter is to educate contractors/vendors on the potential issues that may arise that is considered unethical; which is a result of Chapter 3 Back Room Deals. Federal Acquisition Regulation Part 3 - Improper Business Practices and Personal Conflicts of Interest and United States Title 18 Crimes and Criminal Procedure, Part 1 Crimes, Chapter 11 Bribery, Graft, and Conflicts of Interest. These laws apply to all Federal employees and carry criminal penalties for noncompliance. They also serve as a basis for the ethics regulations known as the Standards of Ethical Conduct for Employees of the Executive Branch, 5 C.F.R. Part 2635.

FAR Part 3 Improper Business Practices and Personal Conflicts of Interest

Solicitation and Acceptance of Gratuities by Government Personnel

As a rule, no Government employee may solicit or accept, directly or indirectly, any gratuity, gift, favor, entertainment, loan, or anything of monetary value from anyone who:

(1) Has or is seeking to obtain Government business with the employee's agency

(2) Conducts activities that are regulated by the employee's agency.

(3) Has interests that may be substantially affected by the performance or nonperformance of the employee's official duties. Certain limited exceptions are authorized in agency regulations.

Bribery of Public Officials Prohibited - 18 U.S.C. § 201

This statute prohibits a Government employee from directly or indirectly receiving or soliciting anything of value in exchange for being influenced in the performance or nonperformance of any official act, including giving testimony, or in exchange for committing fraud.

Restrictions on Compensated Representational Activities - 18 U.S.C. § 203

This statute prohibits a Government employee from seeking or accepting compensation for representational services (rendered either personally or by another) before a Federal court or Government agency in a particular matter in which the United States is a party or has a direct or substantial interest. Representational services include any communications on behalf of another party with the intent to influence the Government. There are limited exceptions, such as for representing oneself or one's immediate family or a person or estate for which the employee acts as a fiduciary, but not where the employee has participated officially or has official responsibility.

Restrictions on Acting as an Agent or Attorney - 18 U.S.C. § 205

This statute prohibits a Government employee from acting as an agent or attorney for anyone before a Federal court or Government agency, whether compensated or not. There are limited exceptions, such as for representing other Federal employees in personnel matters; representing a not-for-profit organization in certain matters, if a majority of its members are current Federal employees or their spouses or dependent children; representing oneself or one's immediate family or a person or estate for which the employee acts as a fiduciary, but not where the employee has participated officially or has official responsibility; or acting as an agent or attorney, in certain matters, for a tribal organization or intertribal consortium to which the employee is assigned under the Intergovernmental Personnel Act or 25 U.S.C. § 48, after advising the Government in writing of any personal and substantial involvement the employee has had in connection with the matter.

Post-Government Employment Restriction - 18 U.S.C. § 207

This statute does not bar an individual, regardless of rank or position, from accepting employment with any private or public employer. It does impose restrictions on certain communications that a former employee may make as a representative of a third party back to the Federal Government. These restrictions are explained more fully in the "Restrictions on Post-Government Employment."

Supplementation of Federal Salary Prohibited - 18 U.S.C. § 209

This statute prohibits a Government employee from receiving any salary, or any contribution to or supplementation of salary; or anything of value from a non-federal entity as compensation for services he or she is expected to perform as a Government employee.

Conflicts of Interest - 18 U.S.C. § 208

This statute prohibits a Government employee from participating personally and substantially, on behalf of the Federal Government, in any particular matter in which he or she has a financial interest. In addition, the statute provides that the financial interests of certain other "persons" are imputed to the employee (that is, the interests are the same as if they were the employee's interests). These other persons include the employee's spouse, minor child, general partner, an organization in which he or she serves as an officer, trustee, partner or employee, and any person or organization with whom the employee is negotiating or has an arrangement concerning future employment. There are limited regulatory exemptions authorized by the Office of Government Ethics, an exception for certain financial interests arising solely out of Native American birthrights, and a very limited waiver authority.

Other Ethical Violations

1. Procurement Integrity
2. Reports of Suspected Antitrust Violations
3. Contingent Fees
4. Other Improper Business Practices

Procurement Integrity

In accordance with FAR Subpart 3.104-3 and Prohibition on disclosing procurement information (41 U.S.C. 2102). This is knowingly disclosing contractor bid or proposal information or source selection information before the award of a Federal agency procurement contract to which the information relates.

Also, prohibition on obtaining procurement information (41 U.S.C. 2102). A person must not, other than as provided by law, knowingly obtain contractor bid or proposal information or source selection information before the award of a Federal agency procurement contract to which the information relates.

- Criminal Penalties: Prison up to 5 years

- Civil Penalties: Not more than $50,000 for each violation plus twice the amount of compensation which the individual received or offered for the prohibited conduct.

- Civil Penalties: An organization that engages in such conduct is subject to a civil penalty of not more than $500,000 for each violation plus twice the amount of compensation which the organization received or offered for the prohibited conduct.

- Administrative Actions:

    (i) Cancellation of the Federal agency procurement, if a contract has not yet been awarded.

    (ii) Rescission of a contract with respect to which—

    (I) the contractor or someone acting for the contractor has been convicted for an offense punishable, or

    (II) The head of the agency that awarded the contract has determined, based upon a preponderance of the evidence that the contractor or someone acting for the contractor has engaged in conduct constituting such an offense.

(iii) Initiation of suspension or debarment proceedings for the protection of the Government in accordance with procedures in the Federal Acquisition Regulation.

- "Suspension" means action taken by a suspending official under 9.407 to disqualify a contractor temporarily from Government contracting and Government-approved subcontracting; a contractor that is disqualified is "suspended."

- "Debarment" means action taken by a debarring official under 9.406 to exclude a contractor from Government contracting and Government-approved subcontracting for a reasonable, specified period; a contractor that is excluded is "debarred."

(iv) Initiation of adverse personnel action, pursuant to the procedures in chapter 75 of title 5 or other applicable law or regulation; which may result in the Government Employee to be:

1. Removed

2. Suspended for more than 14 days

3. Reduction in Grade or Pay, or furlough for 30 days or less.

Reports of Suspected Antitrust Violations

Practices that eliminate competition or restrain trade usually lead to excessive prices and may warrant criminal, civil, or administrative action against the participants. Examples of anticompetitive practices are collusive bidding, follow-the-leader pricing, rotated low bids, collusive price estimating systems, and sharing of the business.

1. Collusive bidding – refers to agreements by contractors or suppliers in a particular trade or area to cooperate to defeat the competitive bidding process in order to inflate prices to artificially high levels. It can occur in large and small contracts.

2. Follow-the-leader pricing – is a competitive pricing strategy, in which a business matches the prices and services of the market leader or pricing strategy in which a player in the particular market tries to follow the pricing strategy of the most dominant player in that segment i.e. if the leader increases the price of good to a particular level the player also increases the price of its good to that level and vice versa.

3. Rotated low bids – competing bidding firms "taking turns" at winning the job. Bid rotation is in effect a form of market allocation where competitors are entitled to their "fair share" of the industry profits.

4. <u>Collusive price estimating systems</u> – this is if multiple companies are using the same estimating system. If the inquiry occurs how each vendor/business does their estimating. The vendor shall accurately describe those policies, procedures, and practices that the Contractor currently uses in preparing cost proposals. If two are alike it may be considered collusive price estimating systems.

5. <u>Sharing of the business</u> – information sharing, employee sharing, profit, etc.

6. <u>Identical Bids</u> – bids for the same line item that are determined to be identical as to unit price or total line item amount, with or without the application of evaluation factors (e.g., discount or transportation cost).

Contingent Fees

Policies and procedures that restrict contingent fee arrangements for soliciting or obtaining Government contracts to those permitted by 10 U.S.C. 2306(b) and 41 U.S.C. 3901.

1. "<u>Bona fide agency</u>" means an established commercial or selling agency, maintained by a contractor for the purpose of securing business, that neither exerts nor proposes to exert improper influence to solicit or obtain Government contracts nor holds itself out as being able to obtain any Government contract or contracts through improper influence.

2. "Bona fide employee" means a person, employed by a contractor and subject to the contractor's supervision and control as to time, place, and manner of performance, who neither exerts nor proposes to exert improper influence to solicit or obtain Government contracts nor holds out as being able to obtain any Government contract or contracts through improper influence.

3. "Contingent fee" means any commission, percentage, brokerage, or other fee that is contingent upon the success that a person or concern has in securing a Government contract.

4. "Improper influence" means any influence that induces or tends to induce a Government employee or officer to give consideration or to act regarding a Government contract on any basis other than the merits of the matter.

Potential Actions:

1. Before Award, rejection of Bid or Proposal.

2. If after award, enforce the Government's right to annul the contract or to recover the fee.

3. Initiate suspension or debarment action.

4. Refer suspected fraudulent or criminal matters to the Department of Justice, as prescribed in agency regulations

Other Improper Business Practices

Buying-In – means submitting an offer below anticipated costs, expecting to

1. Increase the contract amount after award (e.g., through unnecessary or excessively priced change orders); or

2. Receive follow-on contracts at artificially high prices to recover losses incurred on the buy-in contract.

Subcontractor Kickbacks – The Anti-Kickback Act of 1986 (now codified at 41 U.S.C. chapter 87, Kickbacks,) was passed to deter subcontractors from making payments and contractors from accepting payments for the purpose of improperly obtaining or rewarding favorable treatment in connection with a prime contract or a subcontract relating to a prime contract.

"Kickback" means any money, fee, commission, credit, gift, gratuity, thing of value, or compensation of any kind which is provided, to any prime contractor, prime contractor employee, subcontractor, or subcontractor employee for the purpose of improperly obtaining or rewarding favorable treatment in connection with a prime contractor in connection with a subcontract relating to a prime contract.

The Kickback statue prohibits any business or person:

1. Providing, attempting to provide, or offering to provide any kickback.

2. Solicitating, accepting, or attempting to accept any kickback.

3. Including, directly or indirectly, the amount of any kickback in the contract price charged by a subcontractor to a prime contractor or a higher tier subcontractor or in the contract price charged by a prime contractor to the United States.

Unreasonable Restrictions on Subcontractor Sales – Under 10 U.S. Code § 2402 - Prohibition of contractors limiting subcontractor sales directly to the United States. A prime contractor cannot enter into an agreement with a subcontractor which restricts the sales of who the subcontractor may sale too regardless if it is a consumer, business, or Government.

The Government Employee and Contractor can resolve the issues by complying with FAR Part 3, Code of Federal Regulations, and United States Code.

Impartiality in Performing Official Duties - 5 C.F.R. § 2635.502

The Government employee must take appropriate steps to avoid any appearance of loss of impartiality in the performance of your official duties. Beyond the conflict of interest law discussed at 18 U.S.C. § 207, ethics regulations require all employees to recuse themselves from participating in an official matter if their impartiality would be questioned. The regulations identify three circumstances where employees should carefully consider whether their impartiality is subject to question:

1) Where the financial interests of a member of the employee's household would be impacted;

2) If a party or party representative in an official matter has a "covered relationship" with the employee; and

3) Any other time the employee believes his or her impartiality may be subject to question. The term "covered relationship" includes a wide variety of personal and business relationships that an employee or his family members may have with outside parties. Employees who find that a party or representative of a party is a person with whom the employee or a family member has a personal or outside-of-work/unofficial business relationship should consult with their ethics counselor before taking official action in a particular matter.

Contractor & Legal Gifts

If a contractor/vendor or business wishes to gift an item to the Contract Specialist or Contracting Officer, it shall conform to requirements of 5 CFR 2635.204; which are the exceptions to the prohibition for acceptance of gifts.

- Gifts of $20 or less.

- An employee may accept unsolicited gifts having an aggregate market value of $20 or less per source per occasion, provided that the aggregate market value of individual gifts received from any one person under the authority of this paragraph (a) does not exceed $50 in a calendar year.

- This exception does not apply to gifts of cash or of investment interests such as stock, bonds, or certificates of deposit.

- Where the market value of a gift or the aggregate market value of gifts offered on any single occasion exceeds $20, the employee may not pay the excess value over $20 in order to accept that portion of the gift or those gifts worth $20.

- Where the aggregate value of tangible items offered on a single occasion exceeds $20, the employee may decline any distinct and separate item in order to accept those items aggregating $20 or less.

Chapter 5 - Set-asides

FAR Subpart 6.203 -- Set-Asides for Small Business Concerns.

(a) To fulfill the statutory requirements relating to small business concerns, contracting officers may set aside solicitations to allow only such business concerns to compete. This includes contract actions conducted under the Small Business Innovation Research Program

(b) No separate justification or determination and findings is required under this part to set aside a contract action for small business concerns.

(c) Subpart 19.5 prescribes policies and procedures that shall be followed with respect to set-asides.

Note: The United States Government has Agency Contracting Goals.

Each federal agency has a statutory annual goal for awarding contract dollars to particular groups of contractors. The contracting official is responsible for finding contractors that can do the work and meet the agency's goals.

The combined goals for the federal Government are:

- 23 percent of prime contracts for small businesses
- 5 percent of prime and subcontracts for women-owned small businesses
- 5 percent of prime contracts and subcontracts for small disadvantaged businesses
- 3 percent of prime contracts and subcontracts for HUBZone small businesses
- 3 percent of prime and subcontracts for service-disabled veteran-owned small businesses

Agencies have individual goals for what percent of prime and subcontract dollars should go to small businesses. These agency goals may be different than the federal Government's overall goals. The SBA publishes annual agency contracting goals:

https://www.sba.gov/document/support--agency-contracting-goals

FAR Subpart 6.204 -- Section 8(a) Competition.

To fulfill statutory requirements relating to section 8(a) of the Small Business Act, as amended by Public Law 100-656, contracting officers may limit competition to eligible 8(a) participants (see FAR Subpart 19.8.

FAR Subpart 19.8 -- Contracting with the Small Business Administration (The 8(a) Program)

(a) Section 8(a) of the Small Business Act (15 U.S.C. 637(a)) established a program that authorizes the Small Business Administration (SBA) to enter into all types of contracts with other agencies and award subcontracts for performing those contracts to firms eligible for program participation. This program is the "8(a) Business Development Program," commonly referred to as the "8(a) program." A small business that is accepted into the 8(a) program is known as a "participant." SBA's subcontractors are referred to as "8(a) contractors." As used in this subpart, an 8(a) contractor is an 8(a) participant that is currently performing on a Federal contract or order that was set aside for 8(a) participants.

(b) Contracts may be awarded to the SBA for performance by eligible 8(a) participants on either a **sole source** or competitive basis.

(c) Acting under the authority of the program, the SBA certifies to an agency that SBA is competent and responsible to perform a specific contract. The contracting officer has the discretion to award the contract to the SBA based upon mutually agreeable terms and conditions.

(d) The contracting officer shall comply with 19.203 before deciding to offer an acquisition to a small business concern under the 8(a) program. For acquisitions above the simplified acquisition threshold, the contracting officer shall consider 8(a) set-asides or **sole source awards** before considering small business set-asides.

(e) When SBA has delegated its 8(a)-program contract execution authority to an agency, the contracting officer must refer to its agency supplement or other policy directives for appropriate guidance.

FAR Subpart 19.203 Relationship Among Small Business Programs

(a) There is no order of precedence among the 8(a) Program, HUBZone Program, Service-Disabled Veteran-Owned Small Business Procurement Program, or the Women-Owned Small Business (WOSB) Program.

(b) At or below the simplified acquisition threshold. For acquisitions of supplies or services that have an anticipated dollar value exceeding the micro-purchase threshold, but not exceeding the simplified acquisition threshold, the requirement at 19.502-2(a) to exclusively reserve acquisitions for small business concerns does not preclude the contracting officer from awarding a contract to a small business under the 8(a) Program, HUBZone Program, SDVOSB Program, or WOSB Program.

(c) Above the simplified acquisition threshold. For acquisitions of supplies or services that have an anticipated dollar value exceeding the simplified acquisition threshold definition at 2.101, the contracting officer shall first consider an acquisition for the small business socioeconomic contracting programs (i.e., 8(a), HUBZone, SDVOSB, or WOSB programs) before considering a small business set-aside (see 19.502-2(b)). However, if a requirement has been accepted by the SBA under the 8(a) Program, it must remain in the 8(a) Program unless SBA agrees to its release in accordance with 13 CFR parts 124, 125 and 126.

(d) In determining which socioeconomic program to use for an acquisition, the contracting officer should consider, at a minimum—

(1) Results of market research that was done to determine if there are socioeconomic firms capable of satisfying the agency's requirement; and

(2) Agency progress in fulfilling its small business goals.

(e) Small business set-asides have priority over acquisitions using full and open competition.

No separate justification or determination and findings is required under this part to limit competition to eligible 8(a) participants, unless it is over $22 million a Justification and Approval shall be done. See Chapter 7 - Other Than Full and Open Competition.

Note: Section 501 of Public Law 100-656, the Business Opportunity Development Reform Act of 1988, requires executive agencies having contract actions in excess of $50 million in Fiscal Year 1988 or later to prepare an annual forecast of expected contract opportunities, or classes of contract opportunities that small business concerns, including those owned and controlled by socially and economically disadvantaged individuals, are capable of performing.

FAR Subpart 6.205 – Set-asides for HUBZone Small Business Concerns.

To fulfill the statutory requirements relating to the HUBZone Act of 1997 (15 U.S.C. 631 note), contracting officers in participating agencies may set aside solicitations to allow only qualified HUBZone small business concerns to compete.

No separate justification or determination and findings is required under this part to set aside a contract action for qualified HUBZone small business concerns.

FAR Subpart 19.1306 – HUBZone Sole Source Awards.

(a) A contracting officer shall consider a contract award to a HUBZone small business concern on a sole source basis:

FAR Subpart 6.302-5(a)(2) Full and open competition need not be provided for when:

(i) A statute expressly authorizes or requires that the acquisition be made through another agency or from a specified source, or

(ii) The agency's need is for a brand name commercial item for authorized resale.

Before considering a small business set-aside, provided none of the exclusions at FAR Subpart 19.1304

The Requirements that can be satisfied through award to:

1. Federal Prison Industries, Inc. https://www.unicor.gov/index.aspx
2. AbilityOne - https://www.abilityone.gov/procurement_list/index.html
3. Order under Agency Indefinite-delivery Contracts
4. Federal Supply Schedules

   https://www.gsaadvantage.gov/advantage/main/start_page.do
5. Requirements being completed by 8(a) participants
6. Requirements that do not exceed the micro-purchase threshold (Can be

purchased with a Government Purchase Card aka Credit Card)

    a. Construction - $2,000

    b. Services - $2,500

    c. Supplies- $10,000

7. Requirements for commissary or exchange resale items.

apply; and--

(1) The Contracting Officer does not have a reasonable expectation that offers would be received from <u>two or more HUBZone small business concerns</u>;

(2) The anticipated price of the contract, including options, will not exceed—

    (i) $7 million for a requirement within the North American Industry Classification System (NAICS) codes for manufacturing; or

    (ii) $4 million for a requirement within any other NAICS codes;

(4) The acquisition is greater than the simplified acquisition threshold ($250,000)

HUBZone Historical Sole Source NAICS

NAICS	NAICS Description	Obligated Amount	Number of Contracts
115310	SUPPORT ACTIVITIES FOR FORESTRY	$ 332,668.32	11
237120	OIL AND GAS PIPELINE AND RELATED STRUCTURES CONSTRUCTION	$ 6,418,047.19	24
237130	POWER AND COMMUNICATION LINE AND RELATED STRUCTURES CONSTRUCTION	$ 1,465,042.33	2
237310	HIGHWAY, STREET, AND BRIDGE CONSTRUCTION	$ 1,129,334.50	2

NAICS	NAICS Description	Obligated Amount	Number of Contracts
237990	OTHER HEAVY AND CIVIL ENGINEERING CONSTRUCTION	$ 508,377.00	1
238110	POURED CONCRETE FOUNDATION AND STRUCTURE CONTRACTORS	$ 22,875.00	1
238160	ROOFING CONTRACTORS	$ 49,225.42	1
238210	ELECTRICAL CONTRACTORS AND OTHER WIRING INSTALLATION CONTRACTORS	$ 2,726,741.79	6
238290	OTHER BUILDING EQUIPMENT CONTRACTORS	$ 5,500.00	1
238320	PAINTING AND WALL COVERING CONTRACTORS	$ 1,233,562.75	1
238390	OTHER BUILDING FINISHING CONTRACTORS	$ 570,557.65	1
238990	ALL OTHER SPECIALTY TRADE CONTRACTORS	$ 22,129,382.72	4
315990	APPAREL ACCESSORIES AND OTHER APPAREL MANUFACTURING	$ 35,273.25	2
321920	WOOD CONTAINER AND PALLET MANUFACTURING	$ 108,000.00	1
323111	COMMERCIAL PRINTING (EXCEPT SCREEN AND BOOKS)	$ 8,274.23	1
326130	LAMINATED PLASTICS PLATE, SHEET (EXCEPT PACKAGING), AND SHAPE MANUFACTURING	$ 4,770,729.00	1
326199	ALL OTHER PLASTICS PRODUCT MANUFACTURING	$ 45,926.36	1
332311	PREFABRICATED METAL BUILDING AND COMPONENT MANUFACTURING	$ 155,330.00	1
332510	HARDWARE MANUFACTURING	$ 173,338.06	1
332992	SMALL ARMS AMMUNITION MANUFACTURING	$ 519,310.64	2
332994	SMALL ARMS, ORDNANCE, AND ORDNANCE ACCESSORIES MANUFACTURING	$ 765,113.62	4
332999	ALL OTHER MISCELLANEOUS FABRICATED METAL PRODUCT MANUFACTURING	$ 2,788.96	1

NAICS	NAICS Description	Obligated Amount	Number of Contracts
333618	OTHER ENGINE EQUIPMENT MANUFACTURING	$ 2,089,363.16	4
333924	INDUSTRIAL TRUCK, TRACTOR, TRAILER, AND STACKER MACHINERY MANUFACTURING	$ 63,530.77	1
333999	ALL OTHER MISCELLANEOUS GENERAL-PURPOSE MACHINERY MANUFACTURING	$ 1,652,352.00	1
334111	ELECTRONIC COMPUTER MANUFACTURING	$ 125,406.63	1
334112	COMPUTER STORAGE DEVICE MANUFACTURING	$ 91,448.40	1
334118	COMPUTER TERMINAL AND OTHER COMPUTER PERIPHERAL EQUIPMENT MANUFACTURING	$ 1,462,581.19	3
334220	RADIO AND TELEVISION BROADCASTING AND WIRELESS COMMUNICATIONS EQUIPMENT MANUFACTURING	$ 2,201,380.84	1
334290	OTHER COMMUNICATIONS EQUIPMENT MANUFACTURING	$ 246,169.79	2
336992	MILITARY ARMORED VEHICLE, TANK, AND TANK COMPONENT MANUFACTURING	$ 90,136.14	1
337214	OFFICE FURNITURE (EXCEPT WOOD) MANUFACTURING	$ 65,282.60	2
339111	LABORATORY APPARATUS AND FURNITURE MANUFACTURING	$ 8,910.72	1
339113	SURGICAL APPLIANCE AND SUPPLIES MANUFACTURING	$ 2,199,188.75	2
339114	DENTAL EQUIPMENT AND SUPPLIES MANUFACTURING	$ 807,391.74	1
339999	ALL OTHER MISCELLANEOUS MANUFACTURING	$ 893,461.70	5
423320	BRICK, STONE, AND RELATED CONSTRUCTION MATERIAL MERCHANT WHOLESALERS	$ 36,630.00	1

NAICS	NAICS Description	Obligated Amount	Number of Contracts
423410	PHOTOGRAPHIC EQUIPMENT AND SUPPLIES MERCHANT WHOLESALERS	$ 150,574.04	1
423430	COMPUTER AND COMPUTER PERIPHERAL EQUIPMENT AND SOFTWARE MERCHANT WHOLESALERS	$ 116,266.00	2
423930	RECYCLABLE MATERIAL MERCHANT WHOLESALERS	$ 12,714.89	1
424710	PETROLEUM BULK STATIONS AND TERMINALS	$ 47,392.81	1
443120	COMPUTER AND SOFTWARE STORES	$ 7,600.04	1
484121	GENERAL FREIGHT TRUCKING, LONG-DISTANCE, TRUCKLOAD	$ 811,385.00	1
488119	OTHER AIRPORT OPERATIONS	$ 317,238.96	1
488390	OTHER SUPPORT ACTIVITIES FOR WATER TRANSPORTATION	$ 250,000.00	1
511210	SOFTWARE PUBLISHERS	$ 787,876.27	6
517911	TELECOMMUNICATIONS RESELLERS	$ 856,826.83	4
518210	DATA PROCESSING, HOSTING, AND RELATED SERVICES	$ 436,779.00	1
532120	TRUCK, UTILITY TRAILER, AND RV (RECREATIONAL VEHICLE) RENTAL AND LEASING	$ 957,532.79	1
532490	OTHER COMMERCIAL AND INDUSTRIAL MACHINERY AND EQUIPMENT RENTAL AND LEASING	$ 693,344.79	1
541211	OFFICES OF CERTIFIED PUBLIC ACCOUNTANTS	$ 23,605.68	1
541219	OTHER ACCOUNTING SERVICES	$ 19,700.00	1
541330	ENGINEERING SERVICES	$ 3,780,445.33	5
541370	SURVEYING AND MAPPING (EXCEPT GEOPHYSICAL) SERVICES	$ 175,791.46	1
541511	CUSTOM COMPUTER PROGRAMMING SERVICES	$ 6,464,016.49	5
541512	COMPUTER SYSTEMS DESIGN SERVICES	$ 9,581,477.66	4

NAICS	NAICS Description	Obligated Amount	Number of Contracts
541519	OTHER COMPUTER RELATED SERVICES	$ 4,240,299.53	15
541611	ADMINISTRATIVE MANAGEMENT AND GENERAL MANAGEMENT CONSULTING SERVICES	$ 16,358,919.33	11
541620	ENVIRONMENTAL CONSULTING SERVICES	$ 63,175.00	1
541690	OTHER SCIENTIFIC AND TECHNICAL CONSULTING SERVICES	$ 185,000.00	1
541720	RESEARCH AND DEVELOPMENT IN THE SOCIAL SCIENCES AND HUMANITIES	$ 3,936,652.16	2
541820	PUBLIC RELATIONS AGENCIES	$ 180,424.54	1
541990	ALL OTHER PROFESSIONAL, SCIENTIFIC, AND TECHNICAL SERVICES	$ 1,156,373.10	3
561110	OFFICE ADMINISTRATIVE SERVICES	$ 268,672.77	1
561210	FACILITIES SUPPORT SERVICES	$ 979,627.41	22
561320	TEMPORARY HELP SERVICES	$ 459,976.65	2
561730	LANDSCAPING SERVICES	$ 164,981.84	2
561990	ALL OTHER SUPPORT SERVICES	$ 22,129,382.72	47
562111	SOLID WASTE COLLECTION	$ 209,185.25	11
562119	OTHER WASTE COLLECTION	$ 52,560.00	1
562910	REMEDIATION SERVICES	$ 50,957.60	1
611430	PROFESSIONAL AND MANAGEMENT DEVELOPMENT TRAINING	$ 8,000.00	2
611699	ALL OTHER MISCELLANEOUS SCHOOLS AND INSTRUCTION	$ 13,400.52	1
611710	EDUCATIONAL SUPPORT SERVICES	$ 313,980.00	1
711130	MUSICAL GROUPS AND ARTISTS	$ 656,043.00	1
811212	COMPUTER AND OFFICE MACHINE REPAIR AND MAINTENANCE	$ 483,748.20	3

NAICS	NAICS Description	Obligated Amount	Number of Contracts
811310	COMMERCIAL AND INDUSTRIAL MACHINERY AND EQUIPMENT (EXCEPT AUTOMOTIVE AND ELECTRONIC) REPAIR AND MAINTENANCE	$ 3,195,929.96	2
812332	INDUSTRIAL LAUNDERERS	$ 36,231.00	3
813110	RELIGIOUS ORGANIZATIONS	$ 317,762.40	4
922120	POLICE PROTECTION	$ 370,726.00	1

FAR Subpart 6.206 – Set-asides for Service-Disabled Veteran-Owned Small Business Concerns.

(a) To fulfill the statutory requirements relating to the Veterans Benefits Act of 2003 (15 U.S.C. 657f), contracting officers may set-aside solicitations to allow only service-disabled veteran-owned small business concerns to compete.

(b) No separate justification or determination and findings are required under this part to set aside a contract action for service-disabled veteran-owned small business concerns.

FAR Subpart 19.1406 -- Sole Source Awards to Service-disabled Veteran-owned Small Business Concerns.

(A) A Contracting Officer shall consider a contract award to a Service-disabled Veteran-owned Small Business Concerns on a sole source basis:

FAR Subpart 6.302-5(a)(2) Full and open competition need not be provided for when:

(i) A statute expressly authorizes or requires that the acquisition be made through another agency or from a specified source, or

(ii) The agency's need is for a brand name commercial item for authorized resale.

Before considering a small business set-aside, provided none of the exclusions at FAR Subpart 19.1304

The Requirements that can be satisfied through award to:

1. Federal Prison Industries, Inc. https://www.unicor.gov/index.aspx
2. AbilityOne - https://www.abilityone.gov/procurement_list/index.html
3. Order under Agency Indefinite-delivery Contracts
4. Federal Supply Schedules
   https://www.gsaadvantage.gov/advantage/main/start_page.do
5. Requirements being completed by 8(a) participants
6. Requirements that do not exceed the micro-purchase threshold (Can be purchased with a Government Purchase Card aka Credit Card)
   a. Construction - $2,000
   b. Services - $2,500
   c. Supplies- $10,000
7. Requirements for commissary or exchange resale items.

apply; and--

(1) The contracting officer does not have a reasonable expectation that offers would be received from two or more service-disabled veteran-owned small business concerns;

(2) The anticipated award price of the contract, including options, will not exceed—

    (i) $6.5 million for a requirement within the NAICS codes for manufacturing; or

    (ii) $4 million for a requirement within any other NAICS code;

Veteran Historical Sole Source NAICS

NAICS	NAICS Description	Obligated Amount	Number of Contracts
236220	COMMERCIAL AND INSTITUTIONAL BUILDING CONSTRUCTION	$ 84,728.00	1
238220	PLUMBING, HEATING, AND AIR-CONDITIONING CONTRACTORS	$ 38,895.00	1
325413	IN-VITRO DIAGNOSTIC SUBSTANCE MANUFACTURING	$ 9,097.80	1
333415	AIR-CONDITIONING AND WARM AIR HEATING EQUIPMENT AND COMMERCIAL AND INDUSTRIAL REFRIGERATION EQUIPMENT MANUFACTURING	$ 33,679.00	1
334510	ELECTROMEDICAL AND ELECTROTHERAPEUTIC APPARATUS MANUFACTURING	$ 90,027.00	3
334516	ANALYTICAL LABORATORY INSTRUMENT MANUFACTURING	$ 650,216.00	2
334519	OTHER MEASURING AND CONTROLLING DEVICE MANUFACTURING	$ 12,458.88	1
335312	MOTOR AND GENERATOR MANUFACTURING	$ 110,775.75	1
339112	SURGICAL AND MEDICAL INSTRUMENT MANUFACTURING	$ 592,769.67	7

NAICS	NAICS Description	Obligated Amount	Number of Contracts
339113	SURGICAL APPLIANCE AND SUPPLIES MANUFACTURING	$ 31,512.65	3
485991	SPECIAL NEEDS TRANSPORTATION	$ -	2
541330	ENGINEERING SERVICES	$ 171,059.89	1
541380	TESTING LABORATORIES	$ 20,875.00	1
541611	ADMINISTRATIVE MANAGEMENT AND GENERAL MANAGEMENT CONSULTING SERVICES	$ 289,000.00	1
541714	RESEARCH AND DEVELOPMENT IN BIOTECHNOLOGY (EXCEPT NANOBIOTECHNOLOGY)	$ 6,647.00	1
541990	ALL OTHER PROFESSIONAL, SCIENTIFIC, AND TECHNICAL SERVICES	$ 14,700.00	1
561421	TELEPHONE ANSWERING SERVICES	$ 46,838.40	1
561730	LANDSCAPING SERVICES	$ 439,208.00	1
562211	HAZARDOUS WASTE TREATMENT AND DISPOSAL	$ 245,437.61	1
621112	OFFICES OF PHYSICIANS, MENTAL HEALTH SPECIALISTS	$ -	1
621910	AMBULANCE SERVICES	$ -	1
811310	COMMERCIAL AND INDUSTRIAL MACHINERY AND EQUIPMENT (EXCEPT AUTOMOTIVE AND ELECTRONIC) REPAIR AND MAINTENANCE	$ 49,118.70	2

SDVOSB Historical Sole Source NAICS

NAICS	NAICS Description	Obligated Amount	Number of Contracts
115310	SUPPORT ACTIVITIES FOR FORESTRY	$ 176,997.12	1
212321	CONSTRUCTION SAND AND GRAVEL MINING	$ 7,840.00	1
		Obligated	Number of

NAICS	NAICS Description	Amount	Contracts
213112	SUPPORT ACTIVITIES FOR OIL AND GAS OPERATIONS	$ 74,906.38	1
221122	ELECTRIC POWER DISTRIBUTION	$ 154,864.00	2
236210	INDUSTRIAL BUILDING CONSTRUCTION	$ 2,541,756.00	1
236220	COMMERCIAL AND INSTITUTIONAL BUILDING CONSTRUCTION	$ 30,467,141.92	87
237110	WATER AND SEWER LINE AND RELATED STRUCTURES CONSTRUCTION	$ 936,720.52	3
237120	OIL AND GAS PIPELINE AND RELATED STRUCTURES CONSTRUCTION	$ 10,800.00	1
237130	POWER AND COMMUNICATION LINE AND RELATED STRUCTURES CONSTRUCTION	$ 10,848.00	1
237310	HIGHWAY, STREET, AND BRIDGE CONSTRUCTION	$ 1,059,365.80	3
238140	MASONRY CONTRACTORS	$ 1,959,823.00	1
238160	ROOFING CONTRACTORS	$ 454,842.91	4
238190	OTHER FOUNDATION, STRUCTURE, AND BUILDING EXTERIOR CONTRACTORS	$ 16,490.00	1
238210	ELECTRICAL CONTRACTORS AND OTHER WIRING INSTALLATION CONTRACTORS	$ 3,811,633.02	11
238220	PLUMBING, HEATING, AND AIR-CONDITIONING CONTRACTORS	$ 2,846,935.52	23
238290	OTHER BUILDING EQUIPMENT CONTRACTORS	$ 1,484,581.81	1
238320	PAINTING AND WALL COVERING CONTRACTORS	$ 28,330.00	2
238330	FLOORING CONTRACTORS	$ 56,194.19	3
238350	FINISH CARPENTRY CONTRACTORS	$ 279,096.00	2
238390	OTHER BUILDING FINISHING CONTRACTORS	$ 202,454.20	3
238910	SITE PREPARATION CONTRACTORS	$ 764,738.04	4
238990	ALL OTHER SPECIALTY TRADE CONTRACTORS	$ 150,931.00	1
314999	ALL OTHER MISCELLANEOUS TEXTILE PRODUCT MILLS	$ 109,789.50	2

NAICS	NAICS Description	Obligated Amount	Number of Contracts
315999	OTHER APPAREL ACCESSORIES AND OTHER APPAREL MANUFACTURING	$ 357,362.44	1
325120	INDUSTRIAL GAS MANUFACTURING	$ 19,978.21	1
325320	PESTICIDE AND OTHER AGRICULTURAL CHEMICAL MANUFACTURING	$ 6,831.48	2
325412	PHARMACEUTICAL PREPARATION MANUFACTURING	$ 276,567.42	4
325910	PRINTING INK MANUFACTURING	$ 6,132.13	1
325992	PHOTOGRAPHIC FILM, PAPER, PLATE, AND CHEMICAL MANUFACTURING	$ 184,800.00	2
325998	ALL OTHER MISCELLANEOUS CHEMICAL PRODUCT AND PREPARATION MANUFACTURING	$ 317,745.09	4
332311	PREFABRICATED METAL BUILDING AND COMPONENT MANUFACTURING	$ 6,713,523.42	1
332710	MACHINE SHOPS	$ 50,375.00	1
332722	BOLT, NUT, SCREW, RIVET, AND WASHER MANUFACTURING	$ 38,885.00	2
332812	METAL COATING, ENGRAVING (EXCEPT JEWELRY AND SILVERWARE), AND ALLIED SERVICES TO MANUFACTURERS	$ 16,960.00	1
332911	INDUSTRIAL VALVE MANUFACTURING	$ 8,000.00	1
332992	SMALL ARMS AMMUNITION MANUFACTURING	$ 33,106.20	3
332994	SMALL ARMS, ORDNANCE, AND ORDNANCE ACCESSORIES MANUFACTURING	$ 23,653.66	2
332999	ALL OTHER MISCELLANEOUS FABRICATED METAL PRODUCT MANUFACTURING	$ 67,871.96	2
333111	FARM MACHINERY AND EQUIPMENT MANUFACTURING	$ 25,492.00	1
333120	CONSTRUCTION MACHINERY MANUFACTURING	$ 780,585.15	4
333241	FOOD PRODUCT MACHINERY MANUFACTURING	$ 3,270.00	1

NAICS	NAICS Description	Obligated Amount	Number of Contracts
333314	OPTICAL INSTRUMENT AND LENS MANUFACTURING	$ 405,146.81	4
333319	OTHER COMMERCIAL AND SERVICE INDUSTRY MACHINERY MANUFACTURING	$ 389,014.04	7
333415	AIR-CONDITIONING AND WARM AIR HEATING EQUIPMENT AND COMMERCIAL AND INDUSTRIAL REFRIGERATION EQUIPMENT MANUFACTURING	$ 425,136.10	4
333613	MECHANICAL POWER TRANSMISSION EQUIPMENT MANUFACTURING	$ 180,500.00	1
333914	MEASURING, DISPENSING, AND OTHER PUMPING EQUIPMENT MANUFACTURING	$ 48,211.20	1
333923	OVERHEAD TRAVELING CRANE, HOIST, AND MONORAIL SYSTEM MANUFACTURING	$ 13,140.00	1
333924	INDUSTRIAL TRUCK, TRACTOR, TRAILER, AND STACKER MACHINERY MANUFACTURING	$ 8,952.90	1
333997	SCALE AND BALANCE MANUFACTURING (2007), SCALE AND BALANCE (EXCEPT LABORATORY) MANUFACTURING (2002)	$ 26,176.15	1
334111	ELECTRONIC COMPUTER MANUFACTURING	$ 394,475.95	6
334118	COMPUTER TERMINAL AND OTHER COMPUTER PERIPHERAL EQUIPMENT MANUFACTURING	$ 187,337.52	3
334210	TELEPHONE APPARATUS MANUFACTURING	$ 1,727,518.95	1
334220	RADIO AND TELEVISION BROADCASTING AND WIRELESS COMMUNICATIONS EQUIPMENT MANUFACTURING	$ 793,232.31	4
334290	OTHER COMMUNICATIONS EQUIPMENT MANUFACTURING	$ 366,192.94	3
334310	AUDIO AND VIDEO EQUIPMENT MANUFACTURING	$ 299,961.40	5
334417	ELECTRONIC CONNECTOR MANUFACTURING	$ 66,370.20	1
		Obligated	Number of

NAICS	NAICS Description	Amount	Contracts
334510	ELECTROMEDICAL AND ELECTROTHERAPEUTIC APPARATUS MANUFACTURING	$ 11,634,598.53	48
334511	SEARCH, DETECTION, NAVIGATION, GUIDANCE, AERONAUTICAL, AND NAUTICAL SYSTEM AND INSTRUMENT MANUFACTURING	$ 31,290.00	1
334513	INSTRUMENTS AND RELATED PRODUCTS MANUFACTURING FOR MEASURING, DISPLAYING, AND CONTROLLING INDUSTRIAL PROCESS VARIABLES	$ 389,793.15	2
334515	INSTRUMENT MANUFACTURING FOR MEASURING AND TESTING ELECTRICITY AND ELECTRICAL SIGNALS	$ 80,323.00	1
334516	ANALYTICAL LABORATORY INSTRUMENT MANUFACTURING	$ 2,196,043.33	9
334517	IRRADIATION APPARATUS MANUFACTURING	$ 18,459.35	1
335122	COMMERCIAL, INDUSTRIAL, AND INSTITUTIONAL ELECTRIC LIGHTING FIXTURE MANUFACTURING	$ 25,754.85	1
335220	MAJOR HOUSEHOLD APPLIANCE MANUFACTURING	$ 10,909.00	1
335312	MOTOR AND GENERATOR MANUFACTURING	$ 23,672.70	1
335921	FIBER OPTIC CABLE MANUFACTURING	$ 28,923.95	1
335932	NONCURRENT-CARRYING WIRING DEVICE MANUFACTURING	$ 4,145,584.26	1
336111	AUTOMOBILE MANUFACTURING	$ 450.00	1
336112	LIGHT TRUCK AND UTILITY VEHICLE MANUFACTURING	$ 275,747.70	2
336212	TRUCK TRAILER MANUFACTURING	$ 25,128.00	1
336611	SHIP BUILDING AND REPAIRING	$ 1,204,360.31	2
337122	NONUPHOLSTERED WOOD HOUSEHOLD FURNITURE MANUFACTURING	$ 356,495.08	7
		Obligated	Number of

NAICS	NAICS Description	Amount		Contracts
337127	INSTITUTIONAL FURNITURE MANUFACTURING	$	438,651.38	5
337214	OFFICE FURNITURE (EXCEPT WOOD) MANUFACTURING	$	2,315,978.82	14
339112	SURGICAL AND MEDICAL INSTRUMENT MANUFACTURING	$	12,648,559.64	143
339113	SURGICAL APPLIANCE AND SUPPLIES MANUFACTURING	$	7,792,251.93	138
339114	DENTAL EQUIPMENT AND SUPPLIES MANUFACTURING	$	447,986.28	5
339115	OPHTHALMIC GOODS MANUFACTURING	$	779,732.38	10
339116	DENTAL LABORATORIES	$	121,076.26	2
339920	SPORTING AND ATHLETIC GOODS MANUFACTURING	$	17,611.00	1
339940	OFFICE SUPPLIES (EXCEPT PAPER) MANUFACTURING	$	73,000.00	1
339944	CARBON PAPER AND INKED RIBBON MANUFACTURING	$	45,000.00	1
339999	ALL OTHER MISCELLANEOUS MANUFACTURING	$	4,813.00	1
423430	COMPUTER AND COMPUTER PERIPHERAL EQUIPMENT AND SOFTWARE MERCHANT WHOLESALERS	$	2,124,241.15	6
423450	MEDICAL, DENTAL, AND HOSPITAL EQUIPMENT AND SUPPLIES MERCHANT WHOLESALERS	$	167,516.70	2
423830	INDUSTRIAL MACHINERY AND EQUIPMENT MERCHANT WHOLESALERS	$	58,680.00	2
423850	SERVICE ESTABLISHMENT EQUIPMENT AND SUPPLIES MERCHANT WHOLESALERS	$	54,978.45	1
423860	TRANSPORTATION EQUIPMENT AND SUPPLIES (EXCEPT MOTOR VEHICLE) MERCHANT WHOLESALERS	$	868,184.73	1
483211	INLAND WATER FREIGHT TRANSPORTATION	$	966,080.00	1
		Obligated		**Number of**

NAICS	NAICS Description	Amount		Contracts
484210	USED HOUSEHOLD AND OFFICE GOODS MOVING	$	54,456.73	3
488119	OTHER AIRPORT OPERATIONS	$	12,000.00	1
488310	PORT AND HARBOR OPERATIONS	$	173,001.76	2
492110	COURIERS AND EXPRESS DELIVERY SERVICES	$	136,272.07	1
493110	GENERAL WAREHOUSING AND STORAGE	$	1,044,689.10	3
511210	SOFTWARE PUBLISHERS	$	4,633,724.20	5
517312	WIRELESS TELECOMMUNICATIONS CARRIERS (EXCEPT SATELLITE)	$	3,804,217.98	2
517911	TELECOMMUNICATIONS RESELLERS	$	499,240.21	2
517919	ALL OTHER TELECOMMUNICATIONS	$	43,330.56	1
519130	INTERNET PUBLISHING AND BROADCASTING AND WEB SEARCH PORTALS	$	83,196.15	3
519190	ALL OTHER INFORMATION SERVICES	$	62,499.96	1
524210	INSURANCE AGENCIES AND BROKERAGES	$	26,522.00	1
531210	OFFICES OF REAL ESTATE AGENTS AND BROKERS	$	318,957.78	4
532112	PASSENGER CAR LEASING	$	77,225.90	1
532120	TRUCK, UTILITY TRAILER, AND RV (RECREATIONAL VEHICLE) RENTAL AND LEASING	$	1,965,544.78	2
532210	CONSUMER ELECTRONICS AND APPLIANCES RENTAL	$	154,918.00	1
532310	GENERAL RENTAL CENTERS	$	3,900.00	1
532420	OFFICE MACHINERY AND EQUIPMENT RENTAL AND LEASING	$	192,097.56	1
532490	OTHER COMMERCIAL AND INDUSTRIAL MACHINERY AND EQUIPMENT RENTAL AND LEASING	$	383,961.00	1
541110	OFFICES OF LAWYERS	$	62,375.00	1
541219	OTHER ACCOUNTING SERVICES	$	266,101.36	1
		Obligated		**Number of**

NAICS	NAICS Description	Amount		Contracts
541310	ARCHITECTURAL SERVICES	$	1,674,080.97	5
541330	ENGINEERING SERVICES	$	21,794,491.50	26
541350	BUILDING INSPECTION SERVICES	$	39,830.00	2
541380	TESTING LABORATORIES	$	99,956.85	1
541410	INTERIOR DESIGN SERVICES	$	74,403.96	2
541511	CUSTOM COMPUTER PROGRAMMING SERVICES	$	21,630,976.03	19
541512	COMPUTER SYSTEMS DESIGN SERVICES	$	17,710,272.35	17
541513	COMPUTER FACILITIES MANAGEMENT SERVICES	$	423,107.00	2
541519	OTHER COMPUTER RELATED SERVICES	$	21,257,765.96	50
541611	ADMINISTRATIVE MANAGEMENT AND GENERAL MANAGEMENT CONSULTING SERVICES	$	25,923,649.93	29
541612	HUMAN RESOURCES CONSULTING SERVICES (2007), HUMAN RESOURCES AND EXECUTIVE SEARCH CONSULTING SERVICES (2002)	$	2,846,959.89	2
541613	MARKETING CONSULTING SERVICES	$	145,215.96	1
541614	PROCESS, PHYSICAL DISTRIBUTION, AND LOGISTICS CONSULTING SERVICES	$	1,093,725.82	8
541618	OTHER MANAGEMENT CONSULTING SERVICES	$	293,899.96	2
541620	ENVIRONMENTAL CONSULTING SERVICES	$	39,625.00	2
541690	OTHER SCIENTIFIC AND TECHNICAL CONSULTING SERVICES	$	1,008,802.33	5
541712	RESEARCH AND DEVELOPMENT IN THE PHYSICAL, ENGINEERING, AND LIFE SCIENCES (EXCEPT BIOTECHNOLOGY)	$	1,547,256.14	1
541715	RESEARCH AND DEVELOPMENT IN THE PHYSICAL, ENGINEERING, AND LIFE SCIENCES (EXCEPT NANOTECHNOLOGY AND BIOTECHNOLOGY)	$	1,366,338.30	1
		Obligated		Number of

NAICS	NAICS Description	Amount	Contracts
541810	ADVERTISING AGENCIES	$ 35,000.00	1
541820	PUBLIC RELATIONS AGENCIES	$ 344,564.72	1
541990	ALL OTHER PROFESSIONAL, SCIENTIFIC, AND TECHNICAL SERVICES	$ 12,968,766.98	8
561110	OFFICE ADMINISTRATIVE SERVICES	$ 848,515.20	1
561210	FACILITIES SUPPORT SERVICES	$ 2,977,384.68	11
561320	TEMPORARY HELP SERVICES	$ 5,140,026.36	17
561410	DOCUMENT PREPARATION SERVICES	$ 86,979.00	1
561492	COURT REPORTING AND STENOTYPE SERVICES	$ 9,499.12	1
561612	SECURITY GUARDS AND PATROL SERVICES	$ 4,488,928.47	9
561621	SECURITY SYSTEMS SERVICES (EXCEPT LOCKSMITHS)	$ 99,128.77	3
561710	EXTERMINATING AND PEST CONTROL SERVICES	$ 1,357,795.00	1
561720	JANITORIAL SERVICES	$ 1,144,477.94	10
561730	LANDSCAPING SERVICES	$ 1,718,426.03	10
561920	CONVENTION AND TRADE SHOW ORGANIZERS	$ 6,726.67	1
561990	ALL OTHER SUPPORT SERVICES	$ 82,490.34	2
562111	SOLID WASTE COLLECTION	$ 511,149.35	3
562112	HAZARDOUS WASTE COLLECTION	$ 122,911.20	4
562211	HAZARDOUS WASTE TREATMENT AND DISPOSAL	$ 85,922.16	2
562219	OTHER NONHAZARDOUS WASTE TREATMENT AND DISPOSAL	$ 224,626.00	1
562910	REMEDIATION SERVICES	$ 53,520.00	4
611430	PROFESSIONAL AND MANAGEMENT DEVELOPMENT TRAINING	$ 9,273,178.73	10
611519	OTHER TECHNICAL AND TRADE SCHOOLS	$ 641,547.43	3
611710	EDUCATIONAL SUPPORT SERVICES	$ 494,951.44	1
		Obligated	Number of

NAICS	NAICS Description	Amount	Contracts
621111	OFFICES OF PHYSICIANS (EXCEPT MENTAL HEALTH SPECIALISTS)	$ 6,000.00	2
621112	OFFICES OF PHYSICIANS, MENTAL HEALTH SPECIALISTS	$ 750,577.60	2
621399	OFFICES OF ALL OTHER MISCELLANEOUS HEALTH PRACTITIONERS	$ 480,881.00	1
621511	MEDICAL LABORATORIES	$ 8,748.52	1
621512	DIAGNOSTIC IMAGING CENTERS	$ 1,596,521.42	2
621999	ALL OTHER MISCELLANEOUS AMBULATORY HEALTH CARE SERVICES	$ 223,986.42	1
811212	COMPUTER AND OFFICE MACHINE REPAIR AND MAINTENANCE	$ 518,817.18	3
811213	COMMUNICATION EQUIPMENT REPAIR AND MAINTENANCE	$ 160,480.04	2
811219	OTHER ELECTRONIC AND PRECISION EQUIPMENT REPAIR AND MAINTENANCE	$ 914,022.98	11
811310	COMMERCIAL AND INDUSTRIAL MACHINERY AND EQUIPMENT (EXCEPT AUTOMOTIVE AND ELECTRONIC) REPAIR AND MAINTENANCE	$ 901,894.63	8
811412	APPLIANCE REPAIR AND MAINTENANCE	$ 221,898.00	2
812220	CEMETERIES AND CREMATORIES	$ 432,336.00	2
812930	PARKING LOTS AND GARAGES	$ 597,000.00	2

FAR Subpart 6.207 Set-asides for Economically Disadvantaged Women-owned Small Business (EDWOSB) Concerns or Women-owned Small Business (WOSB) Concerns Eligible under the WOSB Program.

(a) To fulfill the statutory requirements relating to 15 U.S.C. 637(m), contracting officers may set aside solicitations for only EDWOSB concerns or WOSB concerns eligible under the WOSB Program.

(b) No separate justification or determination and findings is required under this part to set aside a contract action for EDWOSB concerns or WOSB concerns eligible under the WOSB Program.

FAR Subpart 19.1506 – Women-Owned Small Business Program Sole Source Awards.

(A) A Contracting Officer shall consider a contract award to a Women-owned Small Business Concerns on a sole source basis:

FAR Subpart 6.302-5(a)(2) Full and open competition need not be provided for when:

(i) A statute expressly authorizes or requires that the acquisition be made through another agency or from a specified source, or

(ii) The agency's need is for a brand name commercial item for authorized resale.

Before considering a small business set-aside, provided none of the exclusions at FAR Subpart 19.1304

The Requirements that can be satisfied through award to:

1. Federal Prison Industries, Inc. https://www.unicor.gov/index.aspx
2. AbilityOne - https://www.abilityone.gov/procurement_list/index.html
3. Order under Agency Indefinite-delivery Contracts
4. Federal Supply Schedules
   https://www.gsaadvantage.gov/advantage/main/start_page.do
5. Requirements being completed by 8(a) participants
6. Requirements that do not exceed the micro-purchase threshold (Can be

purchased with a Government Purchase Card aka Credit Card)

    a. Construction - $2,000

    b. Services - $2,500

    c. Supplies- $10,000

7. Requirements for commissary or exchange resale items.

apply; and--

(1) The acquisition is assigned a NAICS code in which SBA has determined that WOSB concerns are underrepresented in Federal procurement;

NAICS	Description of NAICS	Set-Aside
115310	Support Activities for Forestry	WOSB
221310	Water Supply and Irrigation Systems	WOSB
221320	Sewage Treatment Facilities	WOSB
221330	Steam and Air-Conditioning Supply	WOSB
236115	New Single-Family Housing Construction (except For-Sale Builders)	WOSB
236116	New Multifamily Housing Construction (except For-Sale Builders)	WOSB
236117	New Housing For-Sale Builders	WOSB
236118	Residential Remodelers	WOSB
236210	Industrial Building Construction	WOSB
236220	Commercial and Institutional Building Construction	WOSB
237110	Water and Sewer Line and Related Structures Construction	WOSB
237120	Oil and Gas Pipeline and Related Structures Construction	WOSB
237130	Power and Communication Line and Related Structures Construction	WOSB
237310	Highway, Street, and Bridge Construction	WOSB
NAICS	Description of NAICS	Set-Aside
237990	Other Heavy and Civil Engineering Construction	WOSB
238110	Poured Concrete Foundation and Structure Contractors	WOSB

238120	Structural Steel and Precast Concrete Contractors	WOSB
238130	Framing Contractors	WOSB
238140	Masonry Contractors	WOSB
238150	Glass and Glazing Contractors	WOSB
238160	Roofing Contractors	WOSB
238170	Siding Contractors	WOSB
238190	Other Foundation, Structure, and Building Exterior Contractors	WOSB
238210	Electrical Contractors and Other Wiring Installation Contractors	WOSB
238220	Plumbing, Heating, and Air-Conditioning Contractors	WOSB
238290	Other Building Equipment Contractors	WOSB
238310	Drywall and Insulation Contractors	WOSB
238320	Painting and Wall Covering Contractors	WOSB
238330	Flooring Contractors	WOSB
238340	Tile and Terrazzo Contractors	WOSB
238350	Finish Carpentry Contractors	WOSB
238390	Other Building Finishing Contractors	WOSB
238910	Site Preparation Contractors	WOSB
238990	All Other Specialty Trade Contractors	WOSB
311411	Frozen Fruit, Juice, and Vegetable Manufacturing	WOSB
311412	Frozen Specialty Food Manufacturing	WOSB
311421	Fruit and Vegetable Canning	WOSB
311422	Specialty Canning	WOSB
311423	Dried and Dehydrated Food Manufacturing	WOSB
311811	Retail Bakeries	WOSB
311812	Commercial Bakeries	WOSB
311813	Frozen Cakes, Pies, and Other Pastries Manufacturing	WOSB
311821	Cookie and Cracker Manufacturing	WOSB
NAICS	**Description of NAICS**	**Set-Aside**
311824	Dry Pasta, Dough, and Flour Mixes Manufacturing from Purchased Flour	WOSB
311830	Tortilla Manufacturing	WOSB

NAICS	Description of NAICS	Set-Aside
314110	Carpet and Rug Mills	WOSB
314120	Curtain and Linen Mills	WOSB
314910	Textile Bag and Canvas Mills	WOSB
314994	Rope, Cordage, Twine, Tire Cord, and Tire Fabric Mills	WOSB
314999	All Other Miscellaneous Textile Product Mills	WOSB
315210	Cut and Sew Apparel Contractors	EDWOSB
315220	Men's and Boys' Cut and Sew Apparel Manufacturing	EDWOSB
315240	Women's, Girls', and Infants' Cut and Sew Apparel Manufacturing	EDWOSB
315280	Other Cut and Sew Apparel Manufacturing	EDWOSB
321911	Wood Window and Door Manufacturing	EDWOSB
321912	Cut Stock, Resawing Lumber, and Planning	EDWOSB
321918	Other Millwork (including Flooring)	EDWOSB
321920	Wood Container and Pallet Manufacturing	EDWOSB
321991	Manufactured Home (Mobile Home) Manufacturing	EDWOSB
321992	Prefabricated Wood Building Manufacturing	EDWOSB
321999	All Other Miscellaneous Wood Product Manufacturing	EDWOSB
323111	Commercial Printing (except Screen and Books)	WOSB
323113	Commercial Screen Printing	WOSB
323117	Books Printing	WOSB
323120	Support Activities for Printing	WOSB
324110	Petroleum Refineries	WOSB
324121	Asphalt Paving Mixture and Block Manufacturing	WOSB
324122	Asphalt Shingle and Coating Materials Manufacturing	WOSB
324191	Petroleum Lubricating Oil and Grease Manufacturing	WOSB
324199	All Other Petroleum and Coal Products Manufacturing	WOSB
325910	Printing Ink Manufacturing	EDWOSB
325920	Explosives Manufacturing	EDWOSB
NAICS	**Description of NAICS**	**Set-Aside**
325991	Custom Compounding of Purchased Resins	EDWOSB
325992	Photographic Film, Paper, Plate, and Chemical Manufacturing	EDWOSB

NAICS	Description of NAICS	Set-Aside
325998	All Other Miscellaneous Chemical Product and Preparation Manufacturing	EDWOSB
332311	Prefabricated Metal Building and Component Manufacturing	WOSB
332312	Fabricated Structural Metal Manufacturing	WOSB
332313	Plate Work Manufacturing	WOSB
332321	Metal Window and Door Manufacturing	WOSB
332322	Sheet Metal Work Manufacturing	WOSB
332323	Ornamental and Architectural Metal Work Manufacturing	WOSB
332410	Power Boiler and Heat Exchanger Manufacturing	WOSB
332420	Metal Tank (Heavy Gauge) Manufacturing	WOSB
332431	Metal Can Manufacturing	WOSB
332439	Other Metal Container Manufacturing	WOSB
332510	Hardware Manufacturing	WOSB
332811	Metal Heat Treating	WOSB
332812	Metal Coating, Engraving (except Jewelry and Silverware), and Allied Services to Manufacturers	WOSB
332813	Electroplating, Plating, Polishing, Anodizing, and Coloring	WOSB
332911	Industrial Valve Manufacturing	WOSB
332912	Fluid Power Valve and Hose Fitting Manufacturing	WOSB
332913	Plumbing Fixture Fitting and Trim Manufacturing	WOSB
332919	Other Metal Valve and Pipe Fitting Manufacturing	WOSB
332991	Ball and Roller Bearing Manufacturing	WOSB
332992	Small Arms Ammunition Manufacturing	WOSB
332993	Ammunition (except Small Arms) Manufacturing	WOSB
332994	Small Arms, Ordnance, and Ordnance Accessories Manufacturing	WOSB
332996	Fabricated Pipe and Pipe Fitting Manufacturing	WOSB
332999	All Other Miscellaneous Fabricated Metal Product Manufacturing	WOSB
333111	Farm Machinery and Equipment Manufacturing	WOSB
NAICS	**Description of NAICS**	**Set-Aside**
333112	Lawn and Garden Tractor and Home Lawn and Garden Equipment Manufacturing	WOSB
333120	Construction Machinery Manufacturing	WOSB

333131	Mining Machinery and Equipment Manufacturing	WOSB
333132	Oil and Gas Field Machinery and Equipment Manufacturing	WOSB
333314	Optical Instrument and Lens Manufacturing	EDWOSB
333316	Photographic and Photocopying Equipment Manufacturing	EDWOSB
333318	Other Commercial and Service Industry Machinery Manufacturing	EDWOSB
333413	Industrial and Commercial Fan and Blower and Air Purification Equipment Manufacturing	WOSB
333414	Heating Equipment (except Warm Air Furnaces) Manufacturing	WOSB
333415	Air-Conditioning and Warm Air Heating Equipment and Commercial and Industrial Refrigeration Equipment Manufacturing	WOSB
333511	Industrial Mold Manufacturing	WOSB
333514	Special Die and Tool, Die Set, Jig, and Fixture Manufacturing	WOSB
333515	Cutting Tool and Machine Tool Accessory Manufacturing	WOSB
333517	Machine Tool Manufacturing	WOSB
333519	Rolling Mill and Other Metalworking Machinery Manufacturing	WOSB
333912	Air and Gas Compressor Manufacturing	WOSB
333914	Measuring, Dispensing, and Other Pumping Equipment Manufacturing	WOSB
333921	Elevator and Moving Stairway Manufacturing	WOSB
333922	Conveyor and Conveying Equipment Manufacturing	WOSB
333923	Overhead Traveling Crane, Hoist, and Monorail System Manufacturing	WOSB
333924	Industrial Truck, Tractor, Trailer, and Stacker Machinery Manufacturing	WOSB
333991	Power-Driven Hand tool Manufacturing	WOSB
333992	Welding and Soldering Equipment Manufacturing	WOSB
333993	Packaging Machinery Manufacturing	WOSB
333994	Industrial Process Furnace and Oven Manufacturing	WOSB
333995	Fluid Power Cylinder and Actuator Manufacturing	WOSB
333996	Fluid Power Pump and Motor Manufacturing	WOSB
NAICS	**Description of NAICS**	**Set-Aside**
333997	Scale and Balance Manufacturing	WOSB
333999	All Other Miscellaneous General-Purpose Machinery Manufacturing	WOSB

334210	Telephone Apparatus Manufacturing	EDWOSB
334220	Radio and Television Broadcasting and Wireless Communications Equipment Manufacturing	EDWOSB
334290	Other Communications Equipment Manufacturing	EDWOSB
334510	Electromedical and Electrotherapeutic Apparatus Manufacturing	WOSB
334511	Search, Detection, Navigation, Guidance, Aeronautical, and Nautical System and Instrument Manufacturing	WOSB
334512	Automatic Environmental Control Manufacturing for Residential, Commercial, and Appliance Use	WOSB
334513	Instruments and Related Products Manufacturing for Measuring, Displaying, and Controlling Industrial Process Variables	WOSB
334514	Totalizing Fluid Meter and Counting Device Manufacturing	WOSB
334515	Instrument Manufacturing for Measuring and Testing Electricity and Electrical Signals	WOSB
334516	Analytical Laboratory Instrument Manufacturing	WOSB
334517	Irradiation Apparatus Manufacturing	WOSB
334519	Other Measuring and Controlling Device Manufacturing	WOSB
334613	Blank Magnetic and Optical Recording Media Manufacturing	WOSB
334614	Software and Other Prerecorded Compact Disc, Tape, and Record Reproducing	WOSB
335311	Power, Distribution, and Specialty Transformer Manufacturing	EDWOSB
335312	Motor and Generator Manufacturing	EDWOSB
335313	Switchgear and Switchboard Apparatus Manufacturing	EDWOSB
335314	Relay and Industrial Control Manufacturing	EDWOSB
335911	Storage Battery Manufacturing	EDWOSB
335912	Primary Battery Manufacturing	EDWOSB
335921	Fiber Optic Cable Manufacturing	EDWOSB
335929	Other Communication and Energy Wire Manufacturing	EDWOSB
335931	Current-Carrying Wiring Device Manufacturing	EDWOSB
NAICS	**Description of NAICS**	**Set-Aside**
335932	Noncurrent-Carrying Wiring Device Manufacturing	EDWOSB
335991	Carbon and Graphite Product Manufacturing	EDWOSB

335999	All Other Miscellaneous Electrical Equipment and Component Manufacturing	EDWOSB
336310	Motor Vehicle Gasoline Engine and Engine Parts Manufacturing	WOSB
336320	Motor Vehicle Electrical and Electronic Equipment Manufacturing	WOSB
336330	Motor Vehicle Steering and Suspension Components (except Spring) Manufacturing	WOSB
336340	Motor Vehicle Brake System Manufacturing	WOSB
336350	Motor Vehicle Transmission and Power Train Parts Manufacturing	WOSB
336360	Motor Vehicle Seating and Interior Trim Manufacturing	WOSB
336370	Motor Vehicle Metal Stamping	WOSB
336390	Other Motor Vehicle Parts Manufacturing	WOSB
336991	Motorcycle, Bicycle, and Parts Manufacturing	WOSB
336992	Military Armored Vehicle, Tank, and Tank Component Manufacturing	WOSB
336999	All Other Transportation Equipment Manufacturing	WOSB
337110	Wood Kitchen Cabinet and Countertop Manufacturing	WOSB
337121	Upholstered Household Furniture Manufacturing	WOSB
337122	Nonupholstered Wood Household Furniture Manufacturing	WOSB
337124	Metal Household Furniture Manufacturing	WOSB
337125	Household Furniture (except Wood and Metal) Manufacturing	WOSB
337127	Institutional Furniture Manufacturing	WOSB
337211	Wood Office Furniture Manufacturing	EDWOSB
337212	Custom Architectural Woodwork and Millwork Manufacturing	EDWOSB
337214	Office Furniture (except Wood) Manufacturing	EDWOSB
337215	Showcase, Partition, Shelving, and Locker Manufacturing	EDWOSB
339112	Surgical and Medical Instrument Manufacturing	WOSB
339113	Surgical Appliance and Supplies Manufacturing	WOSB
339114	Dental Equipment and Supplies Manufacturing	WOSB
339115	Ophthalmic Goods Manufacturing	WOSB
339116	Dental Laboratories	WOSB
NAICS	**Description of NAICS**	**Set-Aside**
339910	Jewelry and Silverware Manufacturing	WOSB
339920	Sporting and Athletic Goods Manufacturing	WOSB

339930	Doll, Toy, and Game Manufacturing	WOSB
339940	Office Supplies (except Paper) Manufacturing	WOSB
339950	Sign Manufacturing	WOSB
339991	Gasket, Packing, and Sealing Device Manufacturing	WOSB
339992	Musical Instrument Manufacturing	WOSB
339993	Fastener, Button, Needle, and Pin Manufacturing	WOSB
339994	Broom, Brush, and Mop Manufacturing	WOSB
339995	Burial Casket Manufacturing	WOSB
339999	All Other Miscellaneous Manufacturing	WOSB
483111	Deep Sea Freight Transportation	WOSB
483112	Deep Sea Passenger Transportation	WOSB
483113	Coastal and Great Lakes Freight Transportation	WOSB
483114	Coastal and Great Lakes Passenger Transportation	WOSB
484110	General Freight Trucking, Local	EDWOSB
484121	General Freight Trucking, Long-Distance, Truckload	EDWOSB
484122	General Freight Trucking, Long-Distance, Less Than Truckload	EDWOSB
484210	Used Household and Office Goods Moving	WOSB
484220	Specialized Freight (except Used Goods) Trucking, Local	WOSB
484230	Specialized Freight (except Used Goods) Trucking, Long-Distance	WOSB
488410	Motor Vehicle Towing	WOSB
488490	Other Support Activities for Road Transportation	WOSB
488510	Freight Transportation Arrangement	EDWOSB
488991	Packing and Crating	EDWOSB
488999	All Other Support Activities for Transportation	EDWOSB
493110	General Warehousing and Storage	WOSB
493120	Refrigerated Warehousing and Storage	WOSB
493130	Farm Product Warehousing and Storage	WOSB
NAICS	**Description of NAICS**	**Set-Aside**
493190	Other Warehousing and Storage	WOSB
511110	Newspaper Publishers	WOSB

511120	Periodical Publishers	WOSB
511130	Book Publishers	WOSB
511140	Directory and Mailing List Publishers	WOSB
511191	Greeting Card Publishers	WOSB
511199	All Other Publishers	WOSB
511210	Software Publishers	WOSB
512110	Motion Picture and Video Production	WOSB
512120	Motion Picture and Video Distribution	WOSB
512131	Motion Picture Theaters (except Drive-Ins)	WOSB
512132	Drive-In Motion Picture Theaters	WOSB
512191	Teleproduction and Other Postproduction Services	WOSB
512199	Other Motion Picture and Video Industries	WOSB
512230	Music Publishers	WOSB
512240	Sound Recording Studios	WOSB
512250	Record Production and Distribution	WOSB
512290	Other Sound Recording Industries	WOSB
515111	Radio Networks	WOSB
515112	Radio Stations	WOSB
515120	Television Broadcasting	WOSB
517311	Wired Telecommunications Carriers	EDWOSB
517312	Wireless Telecommunications Carriers (except Satellite)	WOSB
517410	Satellite Telecommunications	WOSB
517911	Telecommunications Resellers	WOSB
517919	All Other Telecommunications	WOSB
518210	Data Processing, Hosting, and Related Services	WOSB
519110	News Syndicates	WOSB
519120	Libraries and Archives	WOSB
NAICS	**Description of NAICS**	**Set-Aside**
519130	Internet Publishing and Broadcasting and Web Search Portals	WOSB
519190	All Other Information Services	WOSB

NAICS	Description of NAICS	Set-Aside
524113	Direct Life Insurance Carriers	WOSB
524114	Direct Health and Medical Insurance Carriers	WOSB
524126	Direct Property and Casualty Insurance Carriers	WOSB
524127	Direct Title Insurance Carriers	WOSB
524128	Other Direct Insurance (except Life, Health, and Medical) Carriers	WOSB
524130	Reinsurance Carriers	WOSB
524210	Insurance Agencies and Brokerages	WOSB
524291	Claims Adjusting	WOSB
524292	Third Party Administration of Insurance and Pension Funds	WOSB
524298	All Other Insurance Related Activities	WOSB
531110	Lessors of Residential Buildings and Dwellings	EDWOSB
531120	Lessors of Nonresidential Buildings (except Miniwarehouses)	EDWOSB
531130	Lessors of Miniwarehouses and Self-Storage Units	EDWOSB
531190	Lessors of Other Real Estate Property	EDWOSB
532111	Passenger Car Rental	WOSB
532112	Passenger Car Leasing	WOSB
532120	Truck, Utility Trailer, and RV (Recreational Vehicle) Rental and Leasing	WOSB
532411	Commercial Air, Rail, and Water Transportation Equipment Rental and Leasing	WOSB
532412	Construction, Mining, and Forestry Machinery and Equipment Rental and Leasing	WOSB
532420	Office Machinery and Equipment Rental and Leasing	WOSB
532490	Other Commercial and Industrial Machinery and Equipment Rental and Leasing	WOSB
541110	Offices of Lawyers	WOSB
541191	Title Abstract and Settlement Offices	WOSB
541199	All Other Legal Services	WOSB
541211	Offices of Certified Public Accountants	WOSB
541213	Tax Preparation Services	WOSB
541214	Payroll Services	WOSB
NAICS	**Description of NAICS**	**Set-Aside**
541219	Other Accounting Services	WOSB
541310	Architectural Services	WOSB

541320	Landscape Architectural Services	WOSB
541330	Engineering Services	WOSB
541340	Drafting Services	WOSB
541350	Building Inspection Services	WOSB
541360	Geophysical Surveying and Mapping Services	WOSB
541370	Surveying and Mapping (except Geophysical) Services	WOSB
541380	Testing Laboratories	WOSB
541410	Interior Design Services	EDWOSB
541420	Industrial Design Services	EDWOSB
541430	Graphic Design Services	EDWOSB
541490	Other Specialized Design Services	EDWOSB
541511	Custom Computer Programming Services	WOSB
541512	Computer Systems Design Services	WOSB
541513	Computer Facilities Management Services	WOSB
541519	Other Computer Related Services	WOSB
541611	Administrative Management and General Management Consulting Services	WOSB
541612	Human Resources Consulting Services	WOSB
541613	Marketing Consulting Services	WOSB
541614	Process, Physical Distribution, and Logistics Consulting Services	WOSB
541618	Other Management Consulting Services	WOSB
541620	Environmental Consulting Services	WOSB
541690	Other Scientific and Technical Consulting Services	WOSB
541713	Research and Development in Nanotechnology	WOSB
541714	Research and Development in Biotechnology (except Nanobiotechnology)	WOSB
541715	Research and Development in the Physical, Engineering, and Life Sciences (except Nanotechnology and Biotechnology)	WOSB
541720	Research and Development in the Social Sciences and Humanities	WOSB
NAICS	**Description of NAICS**	**Set-Aside**
541810	Advertising Agencies	WOSB
541820	Public Relations Agencies	WOSB

NAICS	Description of NAICS	Set-Aside
541830	Media Buying Agencies	WOSB
541840	Media Representatives	WOSB
541850	Outdoor Advertising	WOSB
541860	Direct Mail Advertising	WOSB
541870	Advertising Material Distribution Services	WOSB
541890	Other Services Related to Advertising	WOSB
541910	Marketing Research and Public Opinion Polling	WOSB
541921	Photography Studios, Portrait	WOSB
541922	Commercial Photography	WOSB
541930	Translation and Interpretation Services	WOSB
541940	Veterinary Services	WOSB
541990	All Other Professional, Scientific, and Technical Services	WOSB
561110	Office Administrative Services	EDWOSB
561210	Facilities Support Services	WOSB
561410	Document Preparation Services	EDWOSB
561421	Telephone Answering Services	EDWOSB
561422	Telemarketing Bureaus and Other Contact Centers	EDWOSB
561431	Private Mail Centers	EDWOSB
561439	Other Business Service Centers (including Copy Shops)	EDWOSB
561440	Collection Agencies	EDWOSB
561450	Credit Bureaus	EDWOSB
561491	Repossession Services	EDWOSB
561492	Court Reporting and Stenotype Services	EDWOSB
561499	All Other Business Support Services	EDWOSB
561510	Travel Agencies	WOSB
561520	Tour Operators	WOSB
561591	Convention and Visitors Bureaus	WOSB
NAICS	**Description of NAICS**	**Set-Aside**
561599	All Other Travel Arrangement and Reservation Services	WOSB
561611	Investigation Services	WOSB

NAICS	Description	Set-Aside
561612	Security Guards and Patrol Services	WOSB
561613	Armored Car Services	WOSB
561621	Security Systems Services (except Locksmiths)	WOSB
561622	Locksmiths	WOSB
561710	Exterminating and Pest Control Services	WOSB
561720	Janitorial Services	WOSB
561730	Landscaping Services	WOSB
561740	Carpet and Upholstery Cleaning Services	WOSB
561790	Other Services to Buildings and Dwellings	WOSB
561910	Packaging and Labeling Services	WOSB
561920	Convention and Trade Show Organizers	WOSB
561990	All Other Support Services	WOSB
562111	Solid Waste Collection	EDWOSB
562112	Hazardous Waste Collection	EDWOSB
562119	Other Waste Collection	EDWOSB
562211	Hazardous Waste Treatment and Disposal	WOSB
562212	Solid Waste Landfill	WOSB
562213	Solid Waste Combustors and Incinerators	WOSB
562219	Other Nonhazardous Waste Treatment and Disposal	WOSB
562910	Remediation Services	WOSB
562920	Materials Recovery Facilities	WOSB
562991	Septic Tank and Related Services	WOSB
562998	All Other Miscellaneous Waste Management Services	WOSB
611310	Colleges, Universities, and Professional Schools	WOSB
611410	Business and Secretarial Schools	WOSB
611420	Computer Training	WOSB
611430	Professional and Management Development Training	WOSB
NAICS	**Description of NAICS**	**Set-Aside**
611511	Cosmetology and Barber Schools	EDWOSB
611512	Flight Training	EDWOSB

NAICS	Description of NAICS	Set-Aside
611513	Apprenticeship Training	EDWOSB
611519	Other Technical and Trade Schools	EDWOSB
611610	Fine Arts Schools	WOSB
611620	Sports and Recreation Instruction	WOSB
611630	Language Schools	WOSB
611691	Exam Preparation and Tutoring	WOSB
611692	Automobile Driving Schools	WOSB
611699	All Other Miscellaneous Schools and Instruction	WOSB
611710	Educational Support Services	WOSB
621111	Offices of Physicians (except Mental Health Specialists)	WOSB
621112	Offices of Physicians, Mental Health Specialists	WOSB
621410	Family Planning Centers	WOSB
621420	Outpatient Mental Health and Substance Abuse Centers	WOSB
621491	HMO Medical Centers	WOSB
621492	Kidney Dialysis Centers	WOSB
621493	Freestanding Ambulatory Surgical and Emergency Centers	WOSB
621498	All Other Outpatient Care Centers	WOSB
621511	Medical Laboratories	WOSB
621512	Diagnostic Imaging Centers	WOSB
621910	Ambulance Services	WOSB
621991	Blood and Organ Banks	WOSB
621999	All Other Miscellaneous Ambulatory Health Care Services	WOSB
622110	General Medical and Surgical Hospitals	WOSB
623110	Nursing Care Facilities (Skilled Nursing Facilities)	WOSB
624210	Community Food Services	WOSB
624221	Temporary Shelters	WOSB
624229	Other Community Housing Services	WOSB
NAICS	**Description of NAICS**	**Set-Aside**
624230	Emergency and Other Relief Services	WOSB
624310	Vocational Rehabilitation Services	EDWOSB

NAICS	Description of NAICS	Set-Aside
711211	Sports Teams and Clubs	WOSB
711212	Racetracks	WOSB
711219	Other Spectator Sports	WOSB
711310	Promoters of Performing Arts, Sports, and Similar Events with Facilities	WOSB
711320	Promoters of Performing Arts, Sports, and Similar Events without Facilities	WOSB
711410	Agents and Managers for Artists, Athletes, Entertainers, and Other Public Figures	WOSB
711510	Independent Artists, Writers, and Performers	WOSB
721110	Hotels (except Casino Hotels) and Motels	WOSB
721120	Casino Hotels	WOSB
721191	Bed-and-Breakfast Inns	WOSB
721199	All Other Traveler Accommodation	WOSB
721211	RV (Recreational Vehicle) Parks and Campgrounds	WOSB
721214	Recreational and Vacation Camps (except Campgrounds)	WOSB
722310	Food Service Contractors	EDWOSB
722320	Caterers	EDWOSB
722330	Mobile Food Services	EDWOSB
722511	Full-Service Restaurants	WOSB
722513	Limited-Service Restaurants	WOSB
722514	Cafeterias, Grill Buffets, and Buffets	WOSB
722515	Snack and Nonalcoholic Beverage Bars	WOSB
811111	General Automotive Repair	WOSB
811112	Automotive Exhaust System Repair	WOSB
811113	Automotive Transmission Repair	WOSB
811118	Other Automotive Mechanical and Electrical Repair and Maintenance	WOSB
811121	Automotive Body, Paint, and Interior Repair and Maintenance	WOSB
811122	Automotive Glass Replacement Shops	WOSB
811191	Automotive Oil Change and Lubrication Shops	WOSB
NAICS	**Description of NAICS**	**Set-Aside**
811192	Car Washes	WOSB
811198	All Other Automotive Repair and Maintenance	WOSB

811211	Consumer Electronics Repair and Maintenance	WOSB
811212	Computer and Office Machine Repair and Maintenance	WOSB
811213	Communication Equipment Repair and Maintenance	WOSB
811219	Other Electronic and Precision Equipment Repair and Maintenance	WOSB
811310	Commercial and Industrial Machinery and Equipment (except Automotive and Electronic) Repair and Maintenance	WOSB
811411	Home and Garden Equipment Repair and Maintenance	EDWOSB
811412	Appliance Repair and Maintenance	EDWOSB
811420	Reupholstery and Furniture Repair	EDWOSB
811430	Footwear and Leather Goods Repair	EDWOSB
811490	Other Personal and Household Goods Repair and Maintenance	EDWOSB
812111	Barber Shops	WOSB
812112	Beauty Salons	WOSB
812113	Nail Salons	WOSB
812191	Diet and Weight Reducing Centers	WOSB
812199	Other Personal Care Services	WOSB
812310	Coin-Operated Laundries and Drycleaners	WOSB
812320	Dry-cleaning and Laundry Services (except Coin-Operated)	WOSB
812331	Linen Supply	WOSB
812332	Industrial Launderers	WOSB
812910	Pet Care (except Veterinary) Services	WOSB
812921	Photofinishing Laboratories (except One-Hour)	WOSB
812922	One-Hour Photofinishing	WOSB
812930	Parking Lots and Garages	WOSB
812990	All Other Personal Services	WOSB
813110	Religious Organizations	WOSB
813910	Business Associations	WOSB
NAICS	**Description of NAICS**	**Set-Aside**
813920	Professional Organizations	WOSB
813930	Labor Unions and Similar Labor Organizations	WOSB

| 813940 | Political Organizations | WOSB |
| 813990 | Other Similar Organizations (except Business, Professional, Labor, & Political Org.) | WOSB |

(2) The contracting officer does not have a reasonable expectation that offers would be received from <u>two or more WOSB concerns (including EDWOSB concerns)</u>; and

The anticipated award price of the contract, including options, will not exceed--

(i) $6.5 million for a requirement within the NAICS codes for manufacturing; or

(ii) $4 million for a requirement within any other NAICS codes.

WOSB Historical Sole Source NAICS – No Information Recorded in www.fpds.gov or www.usaspending.gov

FAR Clause 52.244-5 Competition in Subcontracting

(a) The Contractor shall select subcontractors (including suppliers) on a competitive basis to the maximum practical extent consistent with the objectives and requirements of the contract.

(b) If the Contractor is an approved mentor under the Department of Defense Pilot Mentor-Protégé Program (Pub. L. 101-510, section 831 as amended), <u>the Contractor may award subcontracts under this contract on a noncompetitive basis to its protégés</u>.

FAR Subpart 44.204(c) the contracting officer shall, when contracting by negotiation, insert the clause at 52.244-5, Competition in Subcontracting, in solicitations and contracts when the contract amount is expected to exceed the simplified acquisition threshold ($250,000), unless—

(1) A firm-fixed-price contract, awarded on the basis of adequate price competition or whose prices are set by law or regulation, is contemplated; or

(2) A time-and-materials, labor-hour, or architect-engineer contract is contemplated.

SUBPART 219.71 Department of Defense Pilot Mentor-Protégé Program (Pub. L. 101-510, section 831 as amended)

219.7100 Scope.
This subpart implements the Pilot Mentor-Protégé Program (hereafter referred to as the "Program") established under section 831 of the National Defense Authorization Act for Fiscal Year 1991 (Pub. L. 101-510; 10 U.S.C. 2302 note), as amended through December 23, 2016. The purpose of the Program is to provide incentives for DOD contractors to assist protégé firms in enhancing their capabilities and to increase participation of such firms in Government and commercial contracts.

219.7101 Policy.
DOD policy and procedures for implementation of the Program are contained in Appendix I, Policy and Procedures for the DoD Pilot Mentor-Protégé Program.

219.7102 General.
The Program includes—

(a) Mentor firms and protégé firms that meet the criteria in Appendix I, section I-102.

(b) Mentor-protégé agreements that establish a developmental assistance program for a protégé firm.

(c) Incentives that DOD may provide to mentor firms, including:

(1) Reimbursement for developmental assistance costs through—

    (i) A separately priced contract line item on a DOD contract; or

    (ii) A separate contract, upon written determination by the cognizant Component Director, Small Business Programs (SBP), that unusual circumstances justify reimbursement using a separate contract; or

(2) Credit toward applicable subcontracting goals, established under a subcontracting plan negotiated under FAR subpart 19.7 or under the DoD Comprehensive Subcontracting Test Program, for developmental assistance costs that are not reimbursed.

219.7103 Procedures.

219.7103-1 General.

The procedures for application, acceptance, and participation in the Program are in Appendix I, Policy and Procedures for the DoD Pilot Mentor-Protégé Program. The Director, SBP, of each military department or defense agency has the authority to approve contractors as mentor firms, approve mentor-protégé agreements, and forward approved mentor-protégé agreements to the contracting officer when funding is available.

219.7103-2 Contracting officer responsibilities.

Contracting officers must—

(a) Negotiate an advance agreement on the treatment of developmental assistance costs for either credit or reimbursement if the mentor firm proposes such an agreement, or delegate authority to negotiate to the administrative contracting officer (see FAR 31.109).

(b) Modify (without consideration) applicable contract(s) to incorporate the clause at 252.232-7005, Reimbursement of Subcontractor Advance Payments--DoD Pilot Mentor-Protégé Program, when a mentor firm provides advance payments to a protégé firm under the Program and the mentor firm requests reimbursement of advance payments.

(c) Modify (without consideration) applicable contract(s) to incorporate other than customary progress payments for protégé firms in accordance with FAR 32.504(c) if a mentor firm provides such payments to a protégé firm and the mentor firm requests reimbursement.

(d) Modify applicable contract(s) to establish a contract line item for reimbursement of developmental assistance costs if—

    (1) A DOD program manager or the cognizant Component Director, SBP, has made funds available for that purpose; and

    (2) The contractor has an approved mentor-protégé agreement.

(e) Negotiate and award a separate contract for reimbursement of developmental assistance costs only if—

    (1) Funds are available for that purpose;

    (2) The contractor has an approved mentor-protégé agreement; and

    (3) The cognizant Component Director, SBP, has made a determination in accordance with 219.7102(c)(1)(ii).

(f) Not authorize reimbursement for costs of assistance furnished to a protégé firm in excess of $1,000,000 in a fiscal year unless a written determination from the cognizant Component Director, SBP, is obtained.

(g) Advise contractors of reporting requirements in Appendix I.

(h) Provide a copy of the approved Mentor-Protégé agreement to the Defense Contract Management Agency administrative contracting officer responsible for conducting the annual performance review (see Appendix I, Section I-113).

219.7104 Developmental assistance costs eligible for reimbursement or credit.

(a) Developmental assistance provided under an approved mentor-protégé agreement is distinct from, and must not duplicate, any effort that is the normal and expected product of the award and administration of the mentor firm's subcontracts. The mentor firm must accumulate and charge costs associated with the latter in accordance with its approved accounting practices. Mentor firm costs that are eligible for reimbursement are set forth in Appendix I.

(b) Before incurring any costs under the Program, mentor firms must establish the accounting treatment of developmental assistance costs eligible for reimbursement or credit. To be eligible for reimbursement under the Program, the mentor firm must incur the costs not later than September 30, 2021.

(c) If the mentor firm is suspended or debarred while performing under an approved mentor-protégé agreement, the mentor firm may not be reimbursed or credited for developmental assistance costs incurred more than 30 days after the imposition of the suspension or debarment.

(d) Developmental assistance costs, incurred by a mentor firm not later than September 30, 2021, that are eligible for crediting under the Program, may be credited toward subcontracting plan goals as set forth in Appendix I.

219.7105 Reporting.

Mentor and protégé firms must report on the progress made under mentor-protégé agreements as indicated in Appendix I, Section I-112.

219.7106 Performance reviews.

The Defense Contract Management Agency will conduct annual performance reviews of all mentor-protégé agreements as indicated in Appendix I, Section I-113. The determinations made in these reviews should be a major factor in determinations of amounts of reimbursement, if any, that the mentor firm is eligible to receive in the remaining years of the Program participation term under the agreement.

Appendix I

I-100 Purpose.

(a) This Appendix I to 48 CFR Chapter 2 implements the Pilot Mentor-Protégé Program (hereafter referred to as the "Program") established under section 831 of Public Law 101-510, the National Defense Authorization Act for Fiscal Year 1991 (10 U.S.C. 2302 note), as amended through November 25, 2015. The purpose of the Program is to provide incentives to major DOD contractors to furnish eligible small business concerns with assistance designed to—

   (1) Enhance the capabilities of eligible small business concerns to perform as subcontractors and suppliers under DOD contracts and other contracts and subcontracts; and
   (2) Increase the participation of such business concerns as subcontractors and suppliers under DOD contracts, other Federal Government contracts, and commercial contracts.

(b) Under the Program, eligible companies approved as mentor firms will enter into mentor-protégé agreements with eligible protégé firms to provide appropriate developmental assistance to enhance the capabilities of the protégé firms to perform as subcontractors and suppliers. DOD may provide the mentor firm with either cost reimbursement or credit against applicable subcontracting goals established under contracts with DOD or other Federal agencies.

(c) DOD will measure the overall success of the Program by the extent to which the Program results in—

   (1) An increase in the dollar value of contract and subcontract awards to protégé firms (under DOD contracts, contracts awarded by other Federal agencies, and commercial contracts) from the date of their entry into the Program until 2 years after the conclusion of the agreement;

   (2) An increase in the number and dollar value of subcontracts awarded to a protégé firm (or former protégé firm) by its mentor firm (or former mentor firm); and

   (3) An increase in the employment level of protégé firms from the date of entry into the Program until 2 years after the completion of the agreement.

(d) This policy sets forth the procedures for participation in the Program applicable to companies that are interested in receiving—

   (1) Reimbursement through a separate contract line item in a DOD contract or a separate contract with DOD; or
   (2) Credit toward applicable subcontracting goals for costs incurred under the Program.

I-101 Definitions.

I-101.1 Affiliation.

With respect to a relationship between a mentor firm and a protégé firm, a relationship described under 13 CFR 121.103.

I-101.2 Minority institution of higher education.

An institution of higher education with a student body that reflects the composition specified in section 312(b)(3), (4), and (5) of the Higher Education Act of 1965 (20 U.S.C. 1058(b)(3), (4), and (5)).

I-101.3 Nontraditional defense contractor.

An entity that is not currently performing and has not performed any contract or subcontract for DoD that is subject to full coverage under the cost accounting standards prescribed pursuant to 41 U.S.C. 1502 and the regulations implementing such section, for at least the 1-year period preceding the solicitation of sources by DoD for the procurement (10 U.S.C. 2302(9)).

I-101.4 Eligible entity employing the severely disabled.

A business entity operated on a for-profit or nonprofit basis that—

(a) Uses rehabilitative engineering to provide employment opportunities for severely disabled individuals and integrates severely disabled individuals into its workforce;

(b) Employs severely disabled individuals at a rate that averages not less than 20 percent of its total workforce;

(c) Employs each severely disabled individual in its workforce generally on the basis of 40 hours per week; and

(d) Pays not less than the minimum wage prescribed pursuant to section 6 of the Fair Labor Standards Act (29 U.S.C. 206) to those employees who are severely disabled individuals.

I-101.5 Severely disabled individual.

An individual who is blind or severely disabled as defined in 41 U.S.C. 8501.

I-101.6 Women-owned small business.

A small business concern owned and controlled by women as defined in Section 8(d)(3)(D) of the Small Business Act (15 U.S.C. 637(d)(3)(D)).

I-101.7 Service-disabled veteran-owned small business.

A small business concern owned and controlled by service-disabled veterans as defined in section 8(d)(3) of the Small Business Act (15 U.S.C. 637(d)(3)).

I-102 Participant eligibility.

(a) To be eligible to participate as a mentor, an entity must—

(1) Be eligible for the award of Federal contracts;

(2) Demonstrate that it—

(i) Is qualified to provide assistance that will contribute to the purpose of the Program;

(ii) Is of good financial health and character; and

(iii) Is not on a Federal list of debarred or suspended contractors; and

(3) Be capable of imparting value to a protégé firm because of experience gained as a DOD contractor or through knowledge of general business operations and Government contracting, as demonstrated by evidence that such entity—

(i) Received DOD contracts and subcontracts equal to or greater than $100 million during the previous fiscal year;

(ii) Is an other-than-small business, unless a waiver to the small business exception has been obtained from the Director, Small Business Programs (SBP), OUSD(A&S);

(iii) Is a prime contractor to DOD with an active subcontracting plan; or

(iv) Has graduated from the 8(a) Business Development Program and provides documentation of its ability to serve as a mentor.

(b) To be eligible to participate as a protégé, an entity must be—

(1) A small business concern;

(2) Eligible for the award of Federal contracts;

(3) Less than half the Small Business Administration (SBA) size standard for its primary North American Industry Classification System (NAICS) code;

(4) Not owned or managed by individuals or entities that directly or indirectly have stock options or convertible securities in the mentor firm; and

(5) At least one of the following:

(i) A qualified HUBZone small business concern.

(ii) A women-owned small business concern.

(iii) A service-disabled veteran-owned small business concern.

(iv) An entity owned and controlled by an Indian tribe.

(v) An entity owned and controlled by a Native Hawaiian organization.

(vi) An entity owned and controlled by socially and economically disadvantaged individuals.

(vii) A qualified organization employing severely disabled individuals.

(viii) A nontraditional defense contractor.

(ix) An entity that currently provides goods or services in the private sector that are critical to enhancing the capabilities of the defense supplier base and fulfilling key DOD needs.

(c) Mentor firms may rely in good faith on a written representation that the entity meets the requirements of paragraph (b) of this section, except that a mentor firm is required to confirm a protégé's status as a HUBZone small business concern (see FAR 19.703(d)).

(d) If at any time the SBA (or DOD in the case of entities employing severely disabled individuals) determines that a protégé is ineligible, assistance that the mentor firm furnishes to the protégé after the date of the determination may not be considered assistance furnished under the Program.

(e) A mentor firm may not enter into an agreement with a protégé firm if SBA has made a determination of affiliation. If SBA has not made such a determination and if the DoD Office of Small Business Programs (OSBP) has reason to believe, based on SBA's regulations   regarding affiliation, that the mentor firm is affiliated with the protégé firm, then DoD OSBP   will request a determination regarding affiliation from SBA.

(f) A company may not be approved for participation in the Program as a mentor firm if, at the time of requesting participation in the Program, it is currently debarred or suspended from contracting with the Federal Government pursuant to FAR subpart 9.4.

(g) If the mentor firm is suspended or debarred while performing under an approved mentor-protégé agreement, the mentor firm—

(1) May continue to provide assistance to its protégé firms pursuant to approved mentor-protégé agreements entered into prior to the imposition of such suspension or debarment;

(2) May not be reimbursed or take credit for any costs of providing developmental assistance to its protégé firm, incurred more than 30 days after the imposition of such suspension or debarment; and

(3) Must promptly give notice of its suspension or debarment to its protégé firm and the cognizant Component Director, SBP.

I-103 Program duration.

(a) New mentor-protégé agreements may be submitted and approved through September 30, 2018.

(b) Mentors incurring costs prior to September 30, 2021, pursuant to an approved mentor-protégé agreement, may be eligible for—

(1) Credit toward the attainment of its applicable subcontracting goals for unreimbursed costs incurred in providing developmental assistance to its protégé firm(s);

(2) Reimbursement pursuant to the execution of a separately priced contract line item added to a contract; or

(3) Reimbursement pursuant to entering into a separate DOD contract upon determination by the cognizant Component Director, SBP, that unusual circumstances justify using a separate contract.

I-104 Selection of protégé firms.

(a) Mentor firms will be solely responsible for selecting protégé firms that qualify under I-102(b). Mentor firms are encouraged to identify and select concerns that have not previously received significant prime contract awards from DOD or any other Federal agency.

(b) The selection of protégé firms by mentor firms may not be protested, except as in paragraph (c) of this section.

(c) In the event of a protest regarding the size or disadvantaged status of an entity selected to be a protégé firm, the mentor firm must refer the protest to the SBA to resolve in accordance with 13 CFR Part 121 (with respect to size) or 13 CFR Part 124 (with respect to disadvantaged status).

(d) For purposes of the Small Business Act, no determination of affiliation or control (either direct or indirect) may be found between a protégé firm and its mentor firm on the basis that the mentor firm has agreed to furnish (or has furnished) to its protégé firm, pursuant to a mentor-protégé agreement, any form of developmental assistance described in I-106(d).

(e) A protégé firm may not be a party to more than one DOD mentor-protégé agreement at a time, and may only participate in the Program during the 5-year period beginning on the date the protégé firm enters into its first mentor-protégé agreement.

I-105 Mentor approval process.

(a) An entity seeking to participate as a mentor must apply to the cognizant Component Director, SBP, to establish its initial eligibility as a mentor. This application may accompany its initial mentor-protégé agreement.

(b) The application must provide the following information:

(1) A statement that the entity meets the requirements in I-102(a), specifying the criteria in I-102(a)(3) under which the entity is applying.

(2) A summary of the entity's historical and recent activities and accomplishments under its small and disadvantaged business utilization program.

(3) The total dollar amount of DOD contracts and subcontracts that the entity received during the 2 preceding fiscal years. (Show prime contracts and subcontracts separately per year.)

(4) The total dollar amount of all other Federal agency contracts and subcontracts that the entity received during the 2 preceding fiscal years. (Show prime contracts and subcontracts separately per year.)

(5) The total dollar amount of subcontracts that the entity awarded under DOD contracts during the 2 preceding fiscal years.

(6) The total dollar amount of subcontracts that the entity awarded under all other Federal agency contracts during the 2 preceding fiscal years.

(7) The total dollar amount and percentage of subcontracts that the entity awarded to firms qualifying under I-102(b)(5)(i) through (vii) during the 2 preceding fiscal years. (Show DOD subcontract awards separately.) If the entity was required to submit a Summary Subcontract Report (SSR) in the Electronic Subcontracting Reporting System, the request must include copies of the final reports for the 2 preceding fiscal years.

(8) Information on the company's ability to provide developmental assistance to its eligible protégé s.

(c) A template of the mentor application is available at: https://business.defense.gov/Programs/Mentor-Protégé -Program/

(d) Companies that apply for participation and are not approved will be provided the reasons and an opportunity to submit additional information for reconsideration.

I-106 Development of mentor-protégé agreements.

(a) Prospective mentors and their protégé s may choose to execute letters of intent prior to negotiation of mentor-protégé agreements.

(b) The agreements should be structured after completion of a preliminary assessment of the developmental needs of the protégé firm and mutual agreement regarding the developmental assistance to be provided to address those needs and enhance the protégé's ability to perform successfully under contracts or subcontracts.

(c) A mentor firm may not require a protégé firm to enter into a mentor-protégé agreement as a condition for award of a contract by the mentor firm, including a subcontract under a DOD contract awarded to the mentor firm.

(d) The mentor-protégé agreement may provide for the mentor firm to furnish any or all of the following types of developmental assistance:

(1) Assistance by mentor firm personnel in—

    (i) General business management, including organizational management, financial management, and personnel management, marketing, and overall business planning;

    (ii) Engineering and technical matters such as production inventory control and quality assurance; and

    (iii) Any other assistance designed to develop the capabilities of the protégé firm under the developmental program described in I-107(g).

(2) Award of subcontracts to the protégé firm under DOD contracts or other contracts on a noncompetitive basis.

(3) Payment of progress payments for the performance of subcontracts by a protégé firm in amounts as provided for in the subcontract; but in no event may any such progress payment exceed 100 percent of the costs incurred by the protégé firm for the performance of the subcontract. Provision of progress payments by a mentor firm to a protégé firm at a rate other than the customary rate for the firm must be implemented in accordance with FAR 32.504(c).

(4) Advance payments under such subcontracts. The mentor firm must administer advance payments in accordance with FAR Subpart 32.4.

(5) Loans.

(6) Assistance that the mentor firm obtains for the protégé firm from one or more of the following:

    (i) Small Business Development Centers established pursuant to section 21 of the Small Business Act (15 U.S.C. 648).

    (ii) Entities providing procurement technical assistance pursuant to 10 U.S.C. Chapter 142 (Procurement Technical Assistance Centers).

    (iii) Historically Black colleges and universities.

    (iv) Minority institutions of higher education.

    (v) Women's business centers described in section 29 of the Small Business Act (15 U.S.C. 656).

(e) Pursuant to FAR 31.109, approved mentor firms seeking either reimbursement or credit are strongly encouraged to enter into an advance agreement with the contracting officer responsible for determining final indirect cost rates under FAR 42.705. The purpose of the advance agreement is to establish the accounting treatment of the costs of the developmental assistance pursuant to the mentor-protégé agreement prior to the incurring of any costs by the mentor firm. An advance agreement is an attempt by both the Government and the mentor firm to avoid possible subsequent dispute based on questions related to reasonableness, allocability, or allowability of the costs of developmental assistance under the Program. Absent an advance agreement, mentor firms are advised to establish the accounting treatment of such costs and to address the need for any changes to their cost accounting practices that may result from the implementation of a mentor-protégé agreement, prior to incurring any costs, and irrespective of whether costs will be reimbursed or credited.

(f) Developmental assistance provided under an approved mentor-protégé agreement is distinct from, and must not duplicate, any effort that is the normal and expected product of the award and administration of the mentor firm's subcontracts. Costs associated with the latter must be accumulated and charged in accordance with the contractor's approved accounting practices; they are not considered developmental assistance costs eligible for either credit or reimbursement under the Program.

I-107 Elements of a mentor-protégé agreement.

Each mentor-protégé agreement shall contain—

(a) The name, address, e-mail address, and telephone number of the mentor and protégé points of contact;

(b) The NAICS code(s) that represent the contemplated supplies or services to be provided by the protégé firm to the mentor firm and a statement that, at the time the agreement is submitted for approval, the protégé firm does not exceed the size standard in I-102(b)(3);

(c) A statement that the protégé firm is eligible to participate in accordance with I-102(b);

(d) A statement that the mentor is eligible to participate in accordance with I-102(a);

(e) Assurances that—

(1) The mentor firm does not share, directly or indirectly, with the protégé firm ownership or management of the protégé firm;

(2) The mentor firm does not have an agreement, at the time the mentor firm enters into a mentor-protégé agreement, to merge with the protégé firm;

(3) The owners and managers of the mentor firm are not the parent, child, spouse, sibling, aunt, uncle, niece, nephew, grandparent, grandchild, or first cousin of an owner or manager of the protégé firm;

(4) The mentor firm has not, during the 2-year period before entering into a mentor-protégé agreement, employed any officer, director, principal stock holder, managing member, or key employee of the protégé firm;

(5) The mentor firm has not engaged in a joint venture with the protégé firm during the 2-year period before entering into a mentor-protégé agreement, unless such joint venture was approved by SBA prior to making any offer on a contract;

(6) The mentor firm is not, directly or indirectly, the primary party providing contracts to the protégé firm, as measured by the dollar value of the contracts; and

(7) The SBA has not made a determination of affiliation or control;

(f) A preliminary assessment of the developmental needs of the protégé firm;

(g) A developmental program for the protégé firm, including—

(1) The type of assistance the mentor will provide to the protégé and how that assistance will—

(i) Increase the protégé's ability to participate in DOD, Federal, and/or commercial contracts and subcontracts; and

(ii) Increase small business subcontracting opportunities in industry categories where eligible protégé s or other small business firms are not dominant in the company's vendor base;

(2) Factors to assess the protégé firm's developmental progress under the Program, including specific milestones for providing each element of the identified assistance;

(3) A description of the quantitative and qualitative benefits to DOD from the agreement, if applicable; and

(4) Goals for additional awards for which the protégé firm can compete outside the Program;

(h) The assistance the mentor will provide to the protégé firm in understanding Federal contract regulations, including the FAR and DFARS, after award of a subcontract under the Program, if applicable;

(i) An estimate of the dollar value and type of subcontracts that the mentor firm will award to the protégé firm, and the period of time over which the subcontracts will be awarded;

(j) A statement from the protégé firm indicating its commitment to comply with the requirements for reporting and for review of the agreement during the duration of the agreement and for 2 years thereafter;

(k) A program participation term for the agreement that does not exceed 3 years. Requests for an extension of the agreement for a period not to exceed an additional 2 years are subject to the approval of the cognizant Component Director, SBP. The justification must detail the unusual circumstances that warrant a term in excess of 3 years;

(l) Procedures for the mentor firm to notify the protégé firm in writing at least 30 days in advance of the mentor firm's intent to voluntarily withdraw its participation in the Program. A mentor firm may voluntarily terminate its mentor-protégé agreement(s) only if it no longer wants to be a participant in the Program as a mentor firm. Otherwise, a mentor firm must terminate a mentor-protégé agreement for cause;

(m) Procedures for the mentor firm to terminate the mentor-protégé agreement for cause which provide that—

(1) The mentor firm must furnish the protégé firm a written notice of the proposed termination, stating the specific reasons for such action, at least 30 days in advance of the effective date of such proposed termination;

(2) The protégé firm must have 30 days to respond to such notice of proposed termination, and may rebut any findings believed to be erroneous and offer a remedial program;

(3) Upon prompt consideration of the protégé firm's response, the mentor firm must either withdraw the notice of proposed termination and continue the protégé firm's participation, or issue the notice of termination; and

(4) The decision of the mentor firm regarding termination for cause, conforming with the requirements of this section, will be final and is not reviewable by DoD;

(n) Procedures for a protégé firm to notify the mentor firm in writing at least 30 days in advance of the protégé firm's intent to voluntarily terminate the mentor-protégé agreement;

(o) Additional terms and conditions as may be agreed upon by both parties; and

(p) Signatures and dates for both parties to the mentor-protégé agreement.

I-108 Submission and approval of mentor-protégé agreements.

(a) Upon solicitation or as determined by the cognizant DOD component, mentors will submit—

(1) A mentor application pursuant to I-105, if the mentor has not been previously approved to participate;

(2) A signed mentor-protégé agreement pursuant to I-107;

(3) A statement as to whether the mentor is seeking credit or reimbursement of costs incurred;

(4) The estimated cost of the technical assistance to be provided, broken out per year;

(5) A justification if program participation term is greater than 3 years (Term of agreements may not exceed 5 years); and

(6) For reimbursable agreements, a specific justification for developmental costs in excess of $1,000,000 per year.

(b) When seeking reimbursement of costs, cognizant DOD components may require additional information.

(c) The mentor-protégé agreement must be approved by the cognizant Component Director, SBP, prior to incurring costs eligible for credit.

(d) The cognizant DOD component will execute a contract modification or a separate contract, if justified pursuant to I-103(b)(3), prior to the mentor's incurring costs eligible for reimbursement.

(e) Credit agreements that are not associated with an existing DoD program and/or component will be submitted for approval to Director, SBP, Defense Contract Management Agency (DCMA), via the mentor's cognizant administrative contracting officer.

(f) A prospective mentor that has identified Program funds to be made available from a DOD program manager must provide the information in paragraph (a) of this section through the program manager to the cognizant Component Director, SBP, with a letter signed by the program manager indicating the amount of funding that has been identified for the developmental assistance program.

I-109 Reimbursement agreements.

The following provisions apply to all reimbursable mentor-protégé agreements:

(a) Assistance provided in the form of progress payments to a protégé firm in excess of the customary progress payment rate for the firm will be reimbursed only if implemented in accordance with FAR 32.504(c).

(b) Assistance provided in the form of advance payments will be reimbursed only if the payments have been provided to a protégé firm under subcontract terms and conditions similar to those in the clause at FAR 52.232-12, Advance Payments. Reimbursement of any advance payments will be made pursuant to the inclusion of the clause at DFARS 252.232-7005, Reimbursement of Subcontractor Advance Payments--DoD Pilot Mentor-Protégé Program, in appropriate contracts. In requesting reimbursement, the mentor firm agrees that the risk of any financial loss due to the failure or inability of a protégé firm to repay any unliquidated advance payments will be the sole responsibility of the mentor firm.

(c) The primary forms of developmental assistance authorized for reimbursement under the Program are identified in I-106(d). On a case-by-case basis, Component Directors, SBP, at their discretion, may approve additional incidental expenses for reimbursement, provided these expenses do not exceed 10 percent of the total estimated cost of the agreement.

(d) The total amount reimbursed to a mentor firm for costs of assistance furnished to a protégé firm in a fiscal year may not exceed $1,000,000 unless the cognizant Component Director, SBP, determines in writing that unusual circumstances justify reimbursement at a higher amount. Request for authority to reimburse in excess of $1,000,000 must detail the unusual circumstances and must be endorsed and submitted by the program manager to the cognizant Component Director, SBP.

(e) DoD may not reimburse any fee to the mentor firm for services provided to the protégé firm pursuant to I-106(d)(6) or for business development expenses incurred by the mentor firm under a contract awarded to the mentor firm while participating in a joint venture with the protégé firm.

(f) Developmental assistance costs that are incurred pursuant to an approved reimbursable mentor-protégé agreement, and have been charged to, but not reimbursed through, a separate contract, or through a separately priced contract line item added to a DoD contract, will not be otherwise reimbursed, as either a direct or indirect cost, under any other DoD contract, irrespective of whether the costs have been recognized for credit against applicable subcontracting goals.

I-110 Credit agreements.

I-110.1 Program provisions applicable to credit agreements.

(a) Developmental assistance costs incurred by a mentor firm for providing assistance to a protégé firm pursuant to an approved credit mentor-protégé agreement may be credited as if the costs were incurred under a subcontract award to that protégé, for the purpose of determining the performance of the mentor firm in attaining an applicable subcontracting goal established under any contract containing a subcontracting plan pursuant to the clause at FAR 52.219-9, Small Business Subcontracting Plan, or the provisions of the DoD Test

Program for Negotiation of Comprehensive Small Business Subcontracting Plans. Unreimbursed developmental assistance costs incurred for a protégé firm that is an eligible entity employing severely disabled individuals may be credited toward the mentor firm's small disadvantaged business subcontracting goal, even if the protégé firm is not a small disadvantaged business concern.

(b) Costs that have been reimbursed through inclusion in indirect expense pools may also be credited as subcontract awards for determining the performance of the mentor firm in attaining an applicable subcontracting goal established under any contract containing a subcontracting plan. However, costs that have not been reimbursed because they are not reasonable, allocable, or allowable will not be recognized for crediting purposes.

(c) Other costs that are not eligible for reimbursement pursuant to I-106(d) may be recognized for credit only if requested, identified, and incorporated in an approved mentor-protégé agreement.

(d) The amount of credit a mentor firm may receive for any such unreimbursed developmental assistance costs must be equal to—

   (1) Four times the total amount of such costs attributable to assistance provided by small business development centers, historically Black colleges and universities, minority institutions, and procurement technical assistance centers.

   (2) Three times the total amount of such costs attributable to assistance furnished by the mentor's employees.

   (3) Two times the total amount of other such costs incurred by the mentor in carrying out the developmental assistance program.

I-110.2 Credit adjustments.

(a) Adjustments may be made to the amount of credit claimed if the Director, SBP, OUSD(A&S), determines that—

   (1) A mentor firm's performance in the attainment of its subcontracting goals through actual subcontract awards declined from the prior fiscal year without justifiable cause; and

   (2) Imposition of such a limitation on credit appears to be warranted to prevent abuse of this incentive for the mentor firm's participation in the Program.

(b) The mentor firm must be afforded the opportunity to explain the decline in small business subcontract awards before imposition of any such limitation on credit. In making the final decision to impose a limitation on credit, the Director, SBP, OUSD(A&S), must consider—

   (1) The mentor firm's overall small business participation rates (in terms of percentages of subcontract awards and dollars awarded) as compared to the participation rates existing during the 2 fiscal years prior to the firm's admission to the Program;

   (2) The mentor firm's aggregate prime contract awards during the prior 2 fiscal years and the total amount of subcontract awards under such contracts; and

   (3) Such other information the mentor firm may wish to submit.

(c) The decision of the Director, SBP, OUSD(A&S), regarding the imposition of a limitation on credit will be final.

I-111 Agreement terminations.

(a) Mentors and/or protégé s must send a copy of any termination notices to the cognizant Component Director, SBP that approved the agreement, and the DCMA administrative contracting officer responsible for conducting the annual review pursuant to I-113.

(b) For reimbursable agreements, mentors must also send copies of any termination to the program manager and to the contracting officer.

(c) Termination of a mentor-protégé agreement will not impair the obligations of the mentor firm to perform pursuant to its contractual obligations under Government contracts and subcontracts.

(d) Termination of all or part of the mentor-protégé agreement will not impair the obligations of the protégé firm to perform pursuant to its contractual obligations under any contract awarded to the protégé firm by the mentor firm.

(e) Mentors and protégé s will follow provisions of the mentor-protégé agreement developed in compliance with I-107(l) through (n).

I-112 Reporting requirements.

I-112.1 Reporting requirements applicable to Individual Subcontract Reports (ISR), Summary Subcontract Reports (SSR) and Standard Forms 294.

(a) Amounts credited toward applicable subcontracting goal(s) for unreimbursed costs under the Program must be separately identified on the appropriate ISR, SSR or SF 294 from the amounts credited toward the goal(s) resulting from the award of actual subcontracts to protégé firms. The combination of the two must equal the mentor firm's overall accomplishment toward the applicable goal(s).

(b) A mentor firm may receive credit toward the attainment of an applicable subcontracting goal for each subcontract awarded by the mentor firm to an entity that qualifies as a protégé firm pursuant to I-102(b).

I-112.2 Program specific reporting requirements.

(a) Mentors must report on the progress made under active mentor-protégé agreements semiannually for the periods ending March 31st and September 30th throughout the Program participation term of the agreement. The September 30th report must address the entire fiscal year.

(1) Reports are due 30 days after the close of each reporting period.

(2) Each report must include the following data on performance under the mentor-protégé agreement:

(i) Dollars obligated (for reimbursable agreements).

(ii) Expenditures.

(iii) Dollars credited, if any, toward applicable subcontracting goals as a result of developmental assistance provided to the protégé and a copy of the ISR or SF 294 and/or SSR for each contract where developmental assistance was credited.

(iv) Any new awards of subcontracts on a competitive or noncompetitive basis to the protégé firm under DOD contracts or other contracts, including the value of such subcontracts.

(v) All technical or management assistance provided by mentor firm personnel for the purposes described in I-106(d).

(vi) Any extensions, increases in the scope of work, or additional payments not previously reported for prior awards of subcontracts on a competitive or noncompetitive basis to the protégé firm under DOD contracts or other contracts, including the value of such subcontracts.

(vii) The amount of any payment of progress payments or advance payments made to the protégé firm for performance under any subcontract made under the Program.

(viii) Any loans made by the mentor firm to the protégé firm.

(ix) All Federal contracts awarded to the mentor firm and the protégé firm as a joint venture, designating whether the award was a restricted competition or a full and open competition.

(x) Any assistance obtained by the mentor firm for the protégé firm from the entities listed at I-106(d)(6).

(xi) Whether there have been any changes to the terms of the mentor-protégé agreement.

(xii) A narrative describing the following:

    (A) The success assistance provided under I-106(d) has had in addressing the developmental needs of the protégé firm.

    (B) The impact on DOD contracts.
    (C) Any problems encountered.

    (D) Any milestones achieved in the protégé firm's developmental program.

(E) Impact of the agreement in terms of capabilities enhanced, certifications received, and technology transferred.

(3) In accordance with section 861, paragraph (b)(2), of the National Defense Authorization Act for Fiscal Year 2016 (Pub. L. 114-92), the reporting requirements specified in paragraphs (a)(2)(iv) through (a)(2)(xii)(C) of this section apply retroactively to mentor-protégé agreements that were in effect on November 25, 2015. Mentors must submit reports as described in paragraph (a) of this section.

(4) A recommended reporting format and guidance for its submission are available at http://www.acq.osd.mil/osbp/sb/programs/mpp/resources.shtml.

(b) The protégé must provide data, annually by October 31st, on the progress made during the prior fiscal year by the protégé in employment, revenues, and participation in DOD contracts during—

(1) Each fiscal year of the Program participation term; and

(2) Each of the 2 fiscal years following the expiration of the Program participation term.

(c) The protégé report required by paragraph (b) of this section may be provided as part of the mentor report for the period ending September 30th required by paragraph (a) of this section.

(d) Progress reports must be submitted—

(1) For credit agreements, to the cognizant Component Director, SBP, that approved the agreement, and the mentor's cognizant DCMA administrative contracting officer; and

(2) For reimbursable agreements, to the cognizant Component Director, SBP, the contracting officer, the DCMA administrative contracting officer, and the program manager.

I-113 Performance reviews.

(a) DCMA will conduct annual performance reviews of the progress and accomplishments realized under approved mentor-protégé agreements. These reviews must verify data provided on the semiannual reports and must provide information as to—

(1) Whether all costs reimbursed to the mentor firm under the agreement were reasonably incurred to furnish assistance to the protégé in accordance with the mentor-protégé agreement and applicable regulations and procedures; and

(2) Whether the mentor and protégé accurately reported progress made by the protégé in employment, revenues, and participation in DOD contracts during the Program participation term and for 2 fiscal years following the expiration of the Program participation term.

(b) A checklist for annual performance reviews is available at https://business.defense.gov/Programs/Mentor-Protégé -Program/ .

Chapter 6 - Unsolicited proposals

An Unsolicited Proposal allows unique and innovative ideas or approaches that have been developed outside the Government to be made available to Government agencies for use in accomplishment of their missions. Unsolicited proposals are offered with the intent that the Government will enter into a contract with the offeror for research and development or other efforts supporting the Government mission, and often represent a substantial investment of time and effort by the offeror

Before a business pursues an Unsolicited Proposal, review the Broad Agency Announcements, Small Business Innovation Research topics, Small Business Technology

Transfer Research topics, Program Research and Development Announcements, or any other Government-initiated solicitation or program. These programs are competitive, and are separate from an Unsolicited Proposal.

When the new and innovative idea does not fall under topic areas publicized under those programs or techniques, the ideas may be submitted as unsolicited proposals.

- Board Agency Announcements – s a competitive solicitation procedure used to obtain proposals for basic and applied research and that part of development not related to the development of a specific system or hardware procurement.

  o Each agency is different. Open a web browser and search for (Input Government Agency Name) Board Agency Announcements.

- Small Business Innovation Research Topics – highly competitive program that encourages domestic small businesses to engage in Federal Research/Research and Development (R/R&D) that has the potential for commercialization. Through a competitive awards-based program, SBIR enables small businesses to explore their technological potential and provides the incentive to profit from its commercialization. By including qualified small businesses in the nation's R&D arena, high-tech innovation is stimulated, and the United States gains entrepreneurial spirit as it meets its specific research and development needs

- https://www.sbir.gov/sbirsearch/topic/current

- Small Business Technology Transfer Research Topics – research programs as established by law (SBIR/STTR Reauthorization Act of 2011) are intended to meet the following goals: stimulate technological innovation in the private sector; strengthen the role of small business in meeting Federal research and development (R&D) needs; increase the commercial application of Federally-supported research results; foster and encourage participation by socially and economically disadvantaged small business concerns (SBCs) and women-owned business concerns; and improve the return on investment from Federally-funded research for economic and social benefits to the Nation.

    - Department of Defense - https://sbir.defensebusiness.org/?AspxAutoDetectCookieSupport=1

    - Department of Energy – https://science.energy.gov/sbir/

    - Department of Health and Human Services – https://sbir.nih.gov/

    - National Aeronautics and Space Administration – https://sbir.gsfc.nasa.gov/

    - National Science Foundation – https://seedfund.nsf.gov/

- <u>Program Research and Development Announcements</u> – solicitation approach to obtain and select proposals from the private sector for the conduct of research, development, and related activities in the energy field.

  - https://www.energy.gov/eere/ssl/research-development

- <u>Any other Government-Initiated Solicitation or Programs</u> – each agency may have separate programs that would need to be searched to identify those programs.

When the new and innovative idea does not fall under topic areas publicized under those programs or techniques, the ideas may be submitted as unsolicited proposals.

Checklist for Unsolicited Proposal

Meets Standard	FAR Part	Information & Definitions
	15.600	This subpart sets forth policies and procedures concerning the submission, receipt, evaluation, and acceptance or rejection of unsolicited proposals.
	15.601	"Advertising material" means material designed to acquaint the Government with a prospective contractor's present products, services, or potential capabilities, or designed to stimulate the Government's interest in buying such products or services.
	15.601	"Commercial item offer" means an offer of a commercial item that the vendor wishes to see introduced in the Government's supply system as an alternate or a replacement for an existing supply item. This term does not include innovative or unique configurations or uses of commercial items that are being offered for further development and that may be submitted as an unsolicited proposal.
	15.601	Contribution" means a concept, suggestion, or idea presented to the Government for its use with no indication that the source intends to devote any further effort to it on the Government's behalf.

Meets Standard	FAR Part	Information 15.606-1 Receipt and Initial Review
	15.606-1(a)(1)	(1) Is a valid unsolicited proposal, meeting the requirements of 15.603(c);
	15.606-1(a)(2)	(2) Is suitable for submission in response to an existing agency requirement (see 15.602);
	15.606-1(a)(3)	(3) Is related to the agency mission;
	15.606-1(a)(4)	(4) Contains sufficient technical information and cost-related or price-related information for evaluation;
	15.606-1(a)(5)	(5) Has overall scientific, technical, or socioeconomic merit;
	15.606-1(a)(6)	(6) Has been approved by a responsible official or other representative authorized to obligate the offeror contractually; and
	15.606-1(a)(7)	(7) Complies with the marking requirements of 15.609.

Meets Standard	FAR Part	Evaluation Factors FAR Subpart 15.603(c)
	15.603(c)(1)	Be innovative and unique
	15.603(c)(2)	Be independently originated and developed by the offeror
	15.603(c)(3)	Be prepared without Government supervision, endorsement, direction, or direct Government involvement
	15.603(c)(4)	Include sufficient detail to permit a determination that Government support could be worthwhile, and the proposed work could benefit the agency's research and development or other mission responsibilities
	15.603(c)(5)	Not be an advance proposal for a known agency requirement that can be acquired by competitive methods
	15.603(c)(6)	Not address a previously published agency requirement

NOTE: Unsolicited proposals allow unique and innovative ideas or approaches that have been developed outside the Government to be made available to Government agencies for use in accomplishment of their missions. Unsolicited proposals are offered with the intent that the Government will enter into a contract with the offeror for research and development or other efforts supporting the Government mission, and often represent a substantial investment of time and effort by the offeror.

NOTE: Advertising material, commercial item offers, or contributions, as defined in 15.601, or routine correspondence on technical issues, are not unsolicited proposals. See Below.	
15.601	"Advertising material" means material designed to acquaint the Government with a prospective contractor's present products, services, or potential capabilities, or designed to stimulate the Government's interest in buying such products or services.
15.601	"Commercial item offer" means an offer of a commercial item that the vendor wishes to see introduced in the Government's supply system as an alternate or a replacement for an existing supply item. This term does not include innovative or unique configurations or uses of commercial items that are being offered for further development and that may be submitted as an unsolicited proposal.
15.601	Contribution" means a concept, suggestion, or idea presented to the Government for its use with no indication that the source intends to devote any further effort to it on the Government's behalf.

Meets Standard	FAR Part	Evaluation Factors - FAR Subpart 15.606-2
	15.606-2(a)(1)	Unique, innovative and meritorious methods, approaches, or concepts demonstrated by the proposal.
	15.606-2(a)(2)	Overall scientific, technical, or socioeconomic merits of the proposal.
	15.606-2(a)(3)	Potential contribution of the effort to the agency's specific mission
	15.606-2(a)(4)	The offeror's capabilities, related experience, facilities, techniques, or unique combinations of these that are integral factors for achieving the proposal objectives
	15.606-2(a)(5)	The qualifications, capabilities, and experience of the proposed principal investigator, team leader, or key personnel critical to achieving the proposal objectives.
	15.606-2(a)(6)	The realism of the proposed cost.

15.609 -- Limited Use of Data.

(a) An unsolicited proposal may include data that the offeror does not want disclosed to the public for any purpose or used by the Government except for evaluation purposes. If the offeror wishes to restrict the data, the title page must be marked with the following legend:

Use and Disclosure of Data

This proposal includes data that shall not be disclosed outside the Government and shall not be duplicated, used, or disclosed -- in whole or in part -- for any purpose other than to evaluate this proposal. However, if a contract is awarded to this offeror as a result of -- or in connection with -- the submission of these data, the Government shall have the right to duplicate, use, or disclose the data to the extent provided in the resulting contract. This restriction does not limit the Government's right to use information contained in these data if they are obtained from another source without restriction. The data subject to this restriction are contained in Sheets [*insert numbers or other identification of sheets*].

(b) The offeror shall also mark each sheet of data it wishes to restrict with the following legend: Use or disclosure of data contained on this sheet is subject to the restriction on the title page of this proposal.

(c) The agency point of contact shall return to the offeror any unsolicited proposal marked with a legend different from that provided in paragraph (a) of this section. The return letter will state that the proposal cannot be considered because it is impracticable for the Government to comply with the legend and that the agency will consider the proposal if it is resubmitted with the proper legend.

(d) The agency point of contact shall place a cover sheet on the proposal or clearly mark it as follows, unless the offeror clearly states in writing that no restrictions are imposed on the disclosure or use of the data contained in the proposal:

Unsolicited Proposal -- Use of Data Limited

All Government personnel must exercise extreme care to ensure that the information in this proposal is not disclosed to an individual who has not been authorized access to such data in accordance with FAR 3.104 (Procurement Integrity Act) and is not duplicated, used, or disclosed in whole or in part for any purpose other than evaluation of the proposal, without the written permission of the offeror. If a contract is awarded on the basis of this proposal, the terms of the contract shall control disclosure and use. This notice does not limit the Government's right to use information contained in the proposal if it is obtainable from another source without restriction. This is a Government notice, and shall not by itself be construed to impose any liability upon the Government or Government personnel for disclosure or use of data contained in this proposal.

(e) Use the notice in paragraph (d) of this section solely as a manner of handling unsolicited proposals that will be compatible with this subpart. However, do not use this notice to justify withholding of a record, or to improperly deny the public access to a record, where an obligation is imposed by the Freedom of Information Act (5 U.S.C. 552). An offeror should identify trade secrets, commercial or financial information, and privileged or confidential information to the Government (see paragraph (a) of this section).

(f) When an agency receives an unsolicited proposal without any restrictive legend from an educational or nonprofit organization or institution, and an evaluation outside the Government is necessary, the agency point of contact shall –

(1) Attach a cover sheet clearly marked with the legend in paragraph (d) of this section;

(2) Change the beginning of this legend to read "All Government and non-Government personnel . . . . "; and

(3) Require any non-Government evaluator to agree in writing that data in the proposal will not be disclosed to others outside the Government.

(g) If the proposal is received with the restrictive legend (see paragraph (a) of this section), the modified cover sheet shall also be used, and permission shall be obtained from the offeror before release of the proposal for evaluation by non-Government personnel.

(h) When an agency receives an unsolicited proposal with or without a restrictive legend from other than an educational or nonprofit organization or institution, and evaluation by Government personnel outside the agency or by experts outside of the Government is necessary, written permission must be obtained from the offeror before release of the proposal for evaluation. The agency point of contact shall --

    (1) Clearly mark the cover sheet with the legend in paragraph (d) or as modified in paragraph (f) of this section; and

    (2) Obtain a written agreement from any non-Government evaluator stating that data in the proposal will not be disclosed to persons outside the Government.

Note: The example provided below is pulled from the Federal Acquisition Regulation. Each agency may have an example that may be used. Each agency has their own point of contact. All it takes is an e-mail or phone call. Searching is as easy as going to your web browser and putting in "Unsolicited Proposal Army" Or

*"**Unsolicited** Proposal insert agency name here"*

Unsolicitated Propopsal Example Letter

Insert Letter Head Here

To: Customs and Border Protection (CBP)   January 24, 2019
Unsolicited Proposals
Milton V. Slade, Jr.
procurement-ipop@cbp.dhs.gov
202-344-3434

Subject: Unsolicited Proposal IAW FAR Subpart 15.605.

a) Basic information:

(1) Offeror's name:
Address:
Type of Organization:

(2) Names and telephone numbers of technical and business personnel to be contacted for evaluation or negotiation purposes;

Technical Personnel:
Telephone Number:

Negotiation Personnel:
Telephone Number:

(3) Identification of proprietary data to be used only for evaluation purposes:

See attachment: See attached Use and Disclosure of Data.

(4) Names of other Federal, State, or local agencies or parties receiving the proposal or funding the proposed effort.

Agency Level	Agency	Sub-Agency	Point of Contact	Funding Proposed Effort
Federal				
State				
Local				

(5) Date of submission:

(6) Signature of a person authorized to represent and contractually obligate the offeror.

John Doe
Title
Address
E-mail
Phone #

(b) Technical information:

(1) Concise title and abstract (approximately 200 words) of the proposed effort.

(2) A reasonably complete discussion stating the objectives of the effort or activity, the method of approach and extent of effort to be employed, the nature and extent of the anticipated results, and the manner in which the work will help to support accomplishment of the agency's mission:

(3) Names and biographical information on the offeror's key personnel who would be involved, including alternates.

    See Attached Resumes of:
        1.
        2.
        3.
        4.

(4) Type of support needed from the agency; e.g., Government property, or personnel resources.

(c) Supporting information:

(1) Proposed price or total estimated cost for the effort in sufficient detail for meaningful evaluation.

(2) Period of time for which the proposal is valid (a 6-month minimum is suggested):

(3) Type of contract preferred:

(4) Proposed duration of effort:

(5) Brief description of the organization, previous experience, relevant past performance, and facilities to be used:

(6) Other statements, if applicable, about organizational conflicts of interest, security clearances, and environmental impacts.

(7) The names and telephone numbers of agency technical or other agency points of contact already contacted regarding the proposal.

Agency	Point of Contact	Phone #	E-mail

Any questions regarding this Unsolicited Proposal please contact John Doe, 555-555-555, at john.doe@gmail.co

John Doe
Director of Technology

Use and Disclosure of Data

This proposal includes data that shall not be disclosed outside the Government and shall not be duplicated, used, or disclosed -- in whole or in part -- for any purpose other than to evaluate this proposal. However, if a contract is awarded to this offeror as a result of -- or in connection with -- the submission of these data, the Government shall have the right to duplicate, use, or disclose the data to the extent provided in the resulting contract. This restriction does not limit the Government's right to use information contained in these data if they are obtained from another source without restriction. The data subject to this restriction are contained in Sheets [*insert numbers or other identification of sheets*].

Chapter 7 - Other Than Full and Open Competition also known As Sole Source Contracts

Exceptions to Competition in Contracting Act (CICA)

Unless the Full and Open Competition has restriction that are mandated by the FAR for the vendor to be registered in www.sam.gov and have specific small business set-aside. The FAR allows for Other Than Full and Open Competition in FAR Part 6, 8, & 13; which is known as purchasing from one business/company/vendor that requires approval at multiple levels. Other than Full and Open Competition will be provided later in the Chapter.

CICA mandates that any contract expected to be greater than $25,000 must be advertised at least 15 days prior to bid solicitation (there is an exception to this rule). This advertising is intended to increase the number of bidders competing for Government contracts, thereby allowing for full and open competition. CICA required the Government to follow these procedures with limited exceptions; any departure from CICA must be documented and approved by the appropriate Government official.

There are exceptions of the 15-day advertisement known as a synopsizing. Synopsizing is a warning that a solicitation will be posted on www.fbo.gov. The details of the synopsis will provide the title, solicitation number, NAICS Code, Size Standard, Product service Code, location, and short description.

Exceptions to Synopsizing

The limited exceptions are as follows as long as the Contracting Officer determines that:

- FAR Subpart 5.101(a)(1) For proposed contract actions expected to exceed $25,000, by synopsizing in the Government Point of Entry www.fbo.gov

- FAR Subpart 5.101(a)(2) For proposed contract actions expected to exceed $15,000, but not expected to exceed $25,000, by displaying in a public place, or by any appropriate electronic means, an unclassified notice of the solicitation or a copy of the solicitation satisfying the requirements.

- FAR Subpart 5.101(a)(2)(ii) The Contracting Officer need not comply with the display requirements of this section when the exemptions at *5.202(a)(1), (a)(4) through (a)(9), or (a)(11) apply*, when oral solicitations are used, or when providing access to a notice of proposed contract action and solicitation through the www.fbo.gov and the notice permits the public to respond to the solicitation electronically.

- FAR Subpart 5.202(a)(1) The synopsis cannot be worded to preclude disclosure of an agency's needs and such disclosure would compromise the national security (e.g., would result in disclosure of classified information). The fact that a proposed solicitation or contract action contains classified information, or that access to classified matter may be necessary to submit a proposal or perform the contract does not, in itself, justify use of this exception to synopsis.

- FAR Subpart 5.202(a)(2) The proposed contract action is made under the conditions described in Chapter 7 - Other Than Full and Open Competition also known As Sole Source Contracts (or, for purchases conducted using simplified acquisition procedures, if unusual and compelling urgency precludes competition to the maximum extent practicable) and the Government would be seriously injured if the agency complies with the time periods.

- FAR Subpart 5.202(a)(3) The proposed contract action is one for which either the written direction of a foreign Government reimbursing the agency for the cost of the acquisition of the supplies or services for such Government, or the terms of an international agreement or treaty between the United States and a foreign Government, or international organizations, has the effect of requiring that the acquisition shall be from specified source.

- FAR Subpart 5.202(a)(4) The proposed contract action is expressly authorized or required by a statute to be made through another Government agency, including acquisitions from the Small Business Administration (SBA) using the authority of section 8(a) of the Small Business Act, or from a specific source such as a workshop for the blind under the rules of the Committee for the Purchase from the Blind and Other Severely Disabled.

- FAR Subpart 5.202(a)(5) The proposed contract action is for <u>utility services</u> other than <u>telecommunications services</u> and only one source is available.

- FAR Subpart 5.202(a)(6) The proposed contract action is an order placed under Subpart 16.5 ordering under indefinite-delivery contract. When the order contains brand-name specifications shall be justified.

- FAR Subpart 5.202(a)(7) The proposed contract action results from acceptance of a proposal under the Small Business Innovation Development Act of 1982 (Pub. L. 97-219). https://history.nih.gov/research/downloads/PL97-219.pdf

- FAR Subpart 5.202(a)(8) The proposed contract action results from the acceptance of an unsolicited research proposal that demonstrates a unique and innovative concept:

    "Unique and innovative concept" when used relative to an unsolicited research proposal, means that--

       (1) In the opinion and to the knowledge of the Government evaluator, the meritorious proposal--

           (i) Is the product of original thinking submitted confidentially by one source;

           (ii) Contains new, novel, or changed concepts, approaches, or methods;

           (iii) Was not submitted previously by another; and

(iv) Is not otherwise available within the Federal Government.

(2) In this context, the term does not mean that the source has the sole capability of performing the research.

And publication of any notice complying with 5.207 (Preparation and Transmittal) of Synopses would improperly disclose the originality of thought or innovativeness of the proposed research or would disclose proprietary information associated with the proposal. This exception does not apply if the proposed contract action results from an unsolicited research proposal and acceptance is based solely upon the unique capability of the source to perform the particular research services proposed (see 6.302-1(a)(2)(i))

FAR Subpart 6.302-1(a)(2) When the supplies or services required by the agency are available from only one responsible source, or, for DoD, NASA, and the Coast Guard, from only one or a limited number of responsible sources, and no other type of supplies or services will satisfy agency requirements, full and open competition need not be provided for.

(i) Supplies or services may be considered to be available from only one source if the source has submitted an unsolicited research proposal that --

(A) Demonstrates a unique and innovative concept or, demonstrates a unique capability of the source to provide the particular research services proposed;

(B) Offers a concept or services not otherwise available to the Government; and,

(C) Does not resemble the substance of a pending competitive acquisition.

- FAR Subpart 5.202(a)(9) The proposed contract action is made for perishable subsistence supplies, and advance notice is not appropriate or reasonable.

- FAR Subpart 5.202(a)(10) The proposed contract action is made under conditions described in one of the following:

  o 6.302-3 Industrial Mobilization; Engineering, Developmental, or Research Capability; or Expert Services.

  o 6.302-5 Authorized or Required by Statute with regard to brand name commercial items for authorized resale.

  o 6.302-7 Public Interest, and advance notice is not appropriate or reasonable.

- FAR Subpart 5.202(a)(11) The proposed contract action is made under the terms of an existing contract that was previously synopsized in sufficient detail to comply with the requirements of 5.207 (Preparation and Transmittal) with respect to the current proposed contract action.

- FAR Subpart 5.202(a)(12) The proposed contract action is by a Defense agency and the proposed contract action will be made and performed outside the United States and its outlying areas, and only local sources will be solicited. This exception does not apply to proposed contract actions covered by the World Trade Organization Government Procurement Agreement or a Free Trade Agreement.

- FAR Subpart 5.202(a)(13) The proposed contract action--

(i) Is for an amount not expected to exceed the simplified acquisition threshold ($250,000);

(ii) Will be made through a means that provides access to the notice of proposed contract action through the GPE; and

(iii) Permits the public to respond to the solicitation electronically.

- FAR Subpart 5.202(a)(14) The proposed contract action is made under conditions described in 6.302-3 (Industrial Mobilization; Engineering, Developmental, or Research Capability; or Expert Services) with respect to the services of an expert to support the Federal Government in any current or anticipated litigation or dispute.

- FAR Subpart 5.202(b) The head of the agency determines in writing, after consultation with the Administrator for Federal Procurement Policy and the Administrator of the Small Business Administration, that advance notice is not appropriate or reasonable

The Government is authorized to establish or maintain alternative sources; which is authorized under FAR Part 16 Types of Contracts, specifically Subpart 16.5 -- Indefinite-Delivery Contracts. When these alternative sources are developed they are posted like any other solicitation. So, if you hear or read the Government has contracts that no one can propose on. This exception is below.

FAR Subpart 6.202 -- Establishing or Maintaining Alternative Sources.

(a) Agencies may exclude a particular source from a contract action in order to establish or maintain an alternative source or sources for the supplies or services being acquired if the agency head determines that to do so would --

    (1) Increase or maintain competition and likely result in reduced overall costs for the acquisition, or for any anticipated acquisition;

    (2) Be in the interest of national defense in having a facility (or a producer, manufacturer, or other supplier) available for furnishing the supplies or services in case of a national emergency or industrial mobilization;

    (3) Be in the interest of national defense in establishing or maintaining an essential engineering, research, or development capability to be provided by an educational or other nonprofit institution or a federally funded research and development center;

    (4) Ensure the continuous availability of a reliable source of supplies or services;

    (5) Satisfy projected needs based on a history of high demand; or

    (6) Satisfy a critical need for medical, safety, or emergency supplies.

(b)

    (1) Every proposed contract action under the authority of paragraph (a) of this section shall be supported by a determination and findings (D&F) (see Subpart 1.7) signed by the head of the agency or designee. This D&F shall not be made on a class basis.

(2) Technical and requirements personnel are responsible for providing all necessary data to support their recommendation to exclude a particular source.

(3) When the authority in subparagraph (a)(1) of this section is cited, the findings shall include a description of the estimated reduction in overall costs and how the estimate was derived.

Other Than Full and Open Competition also known As Sole Source Contracts

Before Other Than Full and Open Competition can occur, specific processes shall occur. When it comes to purchasing only from One Responsible Source (10 days) a sources sought will be done to allow companies to provide interest or their capabilities when it comes to Only One Responsible Source. On to the most important part of the guidebook and the reason why every contractor, vendor, or businesses purchased this guide book.

FAR Subpart 6.303 – Justifications; which stats a Contracting Officer shall not commence negotiations for a sole source contract, commence negotiations for a contract resulting from an unsolicited proposal, or award any other contract without providing for full and open competition unless the Contracting Officer:

(1) Justifies, if required in 6.302 (Circumstances Permitting Other Than Full and Open Competition), the use of such actions in writing;

(2) Certifies the accuracy and completeness of the justification; and

(3) Obtains the approval required by 6.304 - Approval of the Justification.

(b) The contracting officer shall not award a sole-source contract under the 8(a) authority (15 U.S.C. 637(a)) for an amount exceeding $22 million unless--

    (1) The contracting officer justifies the use of a sole-source contract in writing in accordance with 6.303-2 (content; which will be outlined in Chapter 8 - Write it for the Contracting Officer!)

    (2) The justification is approved by the appropriate official designated at 6.304 (Approval and Justification); and

    (3) The justification and related information are made public after award in accordance with 6.305 (Availability of the Justification).

(c) Technical and requirements personnel are responsible for providing and certifying as accurate and complete necessary data to support their recommendation for other than full and open competition.

(d) Justifications required by paragraph (a) above may be made on an individual or class basis. Any justification for contracts awarded under the authority of 6.302-7 (Public Interest) shall only be made on an individual basis. Whenever a justification is made and approved on a class basis, the contracting officer must ensure that each contract action taken pursuant to the authority of the class justification and approval is within the scope of the class justification and approval and shall document the contract file for each contract action accordingly.

(e) The justifications for contracts awarded under the authority cited in 6.302-2 (Unusual and Compelling Urgency) may be prepared and approved within a reasonable time after contract award when preparation and approval prior to award would unreasonably delay the acquisitions.

FAR Subpart 6.302-1 -- Only One Responsible Source and No Other Supplies or Services Will Satisfy Agency Requirements.

(a) Authority

    (2) When the supplies or services required by the agency are available from only one responsible source, or, for DOD, NASA, and the Coast Guard, from only one or a limited number of responsible sources, and no other type of supplies or services will satisfy agency requirements, full and open competition need not be provided for.

        (i) Supplies or services may be considered to be available from only one source if the source has submitted an unsolicited research proposal that --

            (A) Demonstrates a unique and innovative concept (see definition at 2.101), or, demonstrates a unique capability of the source to provide the particular research services proposed;

            (B) Offers a concept or services not otherwise available to the Government; and,

            (C) Does not resemble the substance of a pending competitive acquisition. (See 10 U.S.C. 2304(d)(1)(A) and 41 U.S.C. 3304(b)(1).)

        (ii) Supplies may be deemed to be available only from the original source in the case of a follow-on contract for the continued development or production of a major system or highly specialized equipment, including major components thereof, when it is likely that award to any other source would result in --

            (A) Substantial duplication of cost to the Government that is not expected to be recovered through competition, or

(B) Unacceptable delays in fulfilling the agency's requirements. (See 10 U.S.C. 2304 (d)(1)(B) or 41 U.S.C. 3304 (b)(2).)

(iii) For DoD, NASA, and the Coast Guard, services may be deemed to be available only from the original source in the case of follow-on contracts for the continued provision of highly specialized services when it is likely that award to any other source would result in--

(A) Substantial duplication of cost to the Government that is not expected to be recovered through competition, or

(B) Unacceptable delays in fulfilling the agency's requirements. (See 10 U.S.C. 2304(d)(1)(B).)

(b) *Application.* This authority shall be used, if appropriate, in preference to the authority in 6.302-7 (Public Interest); it shall not be used when any of the other circumstances is applicable. Use of this authority may be appropriate in situations such as the following (these examples are not intended to be all inclusive and do not constitute authority in and of themselves):

(1) When there is a reasonable basis to conclude that the agency's minimum needs can only be satisfied by --

(i) Unique supplies or services available from only one source or only one supplier with unique capabilities; or,

(ii) For DOD, NASA, and the Coast Guard, unique supplies or services available from only one or a limited number of sources or from only one or a limited number of suppliers with unique capabilities.

(2) The existence of limited rights in data, patent rights, copyrights, or secret processes; the control of basic raw material; or similar circumstances, make the supplies and services available from only one source (however, the mere existence of such rights or circumstances does not in and of itself justify the use of these authorities) (see Part 27 (Patents, Data, and Copyrights)).

(3) When acquiring utility services (see 41.101), circumstances may dictate that only one supplier can furnish the service (see 41.202); or when the contemplated contract is for construction of a part of a utility system and the utility company itself is the only source available to work on the system.

(4) When the agency head has determined in accordance with the agency's standardization program that only specified makes and models of technical equipment and parts will satisfy the agency's needs for additional units or replacement items, and only one source is available.

(c) *Application for brand name descriptions.*

(1) An acquisition or portion of an acquisition that uses a brand-name description or other purchase description to specify a particular brand-name, product, or feature of a product, peculiar to one manufacturer—

(i) Does not provide for full and open competition, regardless of the number of sources solicited; and

(ii) Shall be justified and approved in accordance with FAR 6.303 and 6.304.

(A) If only a portion of the acquisition is for a brand-name product or item peculiar to one manufacturer, the justification and approval is to cover only the portion of the acquisition which is brand-name or peculiar to one manufacturer. The justification should state it is covering only the portion of the acquisition which is brand-name or peculiar to one manufacturer, and the approval level requirements will then only apply to that portion;

(B) The justification should indicate that the use of such descriptions in the acquisition or portion of an acquisition is essential to the Government's requirements, thereby precluding consideration of a product manufactured by another company; and

(C) The justification shall be posted with the solicitation (see 5.102(a)(6)).

(2) Brand-name or equal descriptions, and other purchase descriptions that permit prospective contractors to offer products other than those specifically referenced by brand-name, provide for full and open competition and do not require justifications and approvals to support their use.

(d) *Limitations.*

(1) Contracts awarded using this authority shall be supported by the written justifications and approvals described in 6.303 and 6.304.

(2) For contracts awarded using this authority, the notices required by 5.201 shall have been published and any bids, proposals, quotations, or capability statements must have been considered.

FAR Subpart 6.302-2 -- Unusual and Compelling Urgency.

(a) *Authority.*

    (1) Citations: 10 U.S.C. 2304(c)(2) or 41 U.S.C. 3304(a)(2).

    (2) When the agency's need for the supplies or services is of such an unusual and compelling urgency that the Government would be seriously injured unless the agency is permitted to limit the number of sources from which it solicits bids or proposals, full and open competition need not be provided for.

(b) *Application.* This authority applies in those situations where

    (1) An unusual and compelling urgency precludes full and open competition, and

    (2) Delay in award of a contract would result in serious injury, financial or other, to the Government.

(c) *Limitations.*

    (1) Contracts awarded using this authority shall be supported by the written justifications and approvals described in 6.303 and 6.304. These justifications may be made and approved after contract award when preparation and approval prior to award would unreasonably delay the acquisition.

    (2) This statutory authority requires that agencies shall request offers from as many potential sources as is practicable under the circumstances.

(d) *Period of Performance.*

(1) The total period of performance of a contract awarded or modified using this authority—

  (i) May not exceed the time necessary—

    (A) To meet the unusual and compelling requirements of the work to be performed under the contract; and

    (B) For the agency to enter into another contract for the required goods and services through the use of competitive procedures; and

  (ii) May not exceed one year, including all options, unless the head of the agency determines that exceptional circumstances apply. This determination must be documented in the contract file.

(2)

  (i) Any subsequent modification using this authority, which will extend the period of performance beyond one year under this same authority, requires a separate determination. This determination is only required if the cumulative period of performance using this authority exceeds one year. This requirement does not apply to the exercise of options previously addressed in the determination required at (d)(1)(ii) of this section.

  (ii) The determination shall be approved at the same level as the level to which the agency head authority in (d) (1) (ii) of this section is delegated.

(3) The requirements in paragraphs (d) (1) and (d) (2) of this section shall apply to any contract in an amount greater than the simplified acquisition threshold.

(4) The determination of exceptional circumstances is in addition to the approval of the justification in 6.304.

(5) The determination may be made after contract award when making the determination prior to award would unreasonably delay the acquisition.

FAR Subpart 6.302-3 -- Industrial Mobilization; Engineering, Developmental, or Research Capability; or Expert Services.

(a) *Authority.*

(1) Citations: 10 U.S.C. 2304(c)(3) or 41 U.S.C. 3304(a)(3).

(2) Full and open competition need not be provided for when it is necessary to award the contract to a particular source or sources in order--

(i) To maintain a facility, producer, manufacturer, or other supplier available for furnishing supplies or services in case of a national emergency or to achieve industrial mobilization,

(ii) To establish or maintain an essential engineering, research, or development capability to be provided by an educational or other nonprofit institution or a federally funded research and development center, or

(iii) To acquire the services of an expert or neutral person for any current or anticipated litigation or dispute.

(b) *Application.*

(1) Use of the authority in paragraph (a)(2)(i) of this subsection may be appropriate when it is necessary to --

  (i) Keep vital facilities or suppliers in business or make them available in the event of a national emergency;

  (ii) Train a selected supplier in the furnishing of critical supplies or services; prevent the loss of a supplier's ability and employees' skills; or maintain active engineering, research, or development work;

  (iii) Maintain properly balanced sources of supply for meeting the requirements of acquisition programs in the interest of industrial mobilization (when the quantity required is substantially larger than the quantity that must be awarded in order to meet the objectives of this authority, that portion not required to meet such objectives will be acquired by providing for full and open competition, as appropriate, under this part);

  (iv) Create or maintain the required domestic capability for production of critical supplies by limiting competition to items manufactured in--

    (A) The United States or its outlying areas; or

    (B) The United States, its outlying areas, or Canada.

  (v) Continue in production, contractors that are manufacturing critical items, when there would otherwise be a break in production; or

  (vi) Divide current production requirements among two or more contractors to provide for an adequate industrial mobilization base.

(2) Use of the authority in paragraph (a)(2)(ii) of this subsection may be appropriate when it is necessary to --

   (i) Establish or maintain an essential capability for theoretical analyses, exploratory studies, or experiments in any field of science or technology;

   (ii) Establish or maintain an essential capability for engineering or developmental work calling for the practical application of investigative findings and theories of a scientific or technical nature; or

   (iii) Contract for supplies or services as are necessary incident to paragraphs (b)(2)(i) or (ii) of this subsection.

(3) Use of the authority in paragraph (a)(2)(iii) of this subsection may be appropriate when it is necessary to acquire the services of either --

   (i) An expert to use, in any litigation or dispute (including any reasonably foreseeable litigation or dispute) involving the Government in any trial, hearing, or proceeding before any court, administrative tribunal, or agency, whether or not the expert is expected to testify. Examples of such services include, but are not limited to:

      (A) Assisting the Government in the analysis, presentation, or defense of any claim or request for adjustment to contract terms and conditions, whether asserted by a contractor or the Government, which is in litigation or dispute, or is anticipated to result in dispute or litigation before any court, administrative tribunal, or agency, or

(B) Participating in any part of an alternative dispute resolution process, including but not limited to evaluators, fact finders, or witnesses, regardless of whether the expert is expected to testify; or

(ii) A neutral person, *e.g.*, mediators or arbitrators, to facilitate the resolution of issues in an alternative dispute resolution process.

(c) *Limitations.* Contracts awarded using this authority shall be supported by the written justifications and approvals described in 6.303 and 6.304.

FAR Subpart 6.302-4 -- International Agreement.

(a) *Authority.*

(1) Citations: 10 U.S.C. 2304(c)(4) or 41 U.S.C. 3304(a)(4).

(2) Full and open competition need not be provided for when precluded by the terms of an international agreement or a treaty between the United States and a foreign government or international organization, or the written directions of a foreign government reimbursing the agency for the cost of the acquisition of the supplies or services for such government.

(b) *Application.* This authority may be used in circumstances such as --

(1) When a contemplated acquisition is to be reimbursed by a foreign country that requires that the product be obtained from a particular firm as specified in official written direction such as a Letter of Offer and Acceptance; or

(2) When a contemplated acquisition is for services to be performed, or supplies to be used, in the sovereign territory of another country and the terms of a treaty or agreement specify or limit the sources to be solicited.

(c) *Limitations*. Except for DOD, NASA, and the Coast Guard, contracts awarded using this authority shall be supported by written justifications and approvals described in 6.303 and 6.304.

FAR Subpart 6.302-5 -- Authorized or Required by Statute.

(a) *Authority*.

(1) Citations: 10 U.S.C. 2304(c)(5) or 41 U.S.C. 3304(a)(5).

(2) Full and open competition need not be provided for when

(i) A statute expressly authorizes or requires that the acquisition be made through another agency or from a specified source, or

(ii) The agency's need is for a brand name commercial item for authorized resale.

(b) *Application*. This authority may be used when statutes, such as the following, expressly authorize or require that acquisition be made from a specified source or through another agency:

(1) Federal Prison Industries (UNICOR) -- 18 U.S.C. 4124

(2) Qualified Nonprofit Agencies for the Blind or other Severely Disabled -- 41 U.S.C. 85, Committee for Purchase From People Who Are Blind or Severely Disabled (see

(3) Government Printing and Binding -- 44 U.S.C. 501-504, 1121

(4) Sole source awards under the 8(a) Program (15 U.S.C. 637), but see 6.303 for requirements for justification and approval of sole-source 8(a) awards over $22 million.

(5) Sole source awards under the HUBZone Act of 1997—15 U.S.C. 657a

(6) Sole source awards under the Veterans Benefits Act of 2003

(7) Sole source awards under the WOSB Program-15 U.S.C. 637(m)

(c) *Limitations.*

(1) This authority shall not be used when a provision of law requires an agency to award a new contract to a specified non-Federal Government entity unless the provision of law specifically --

(i) Identifies the entity involved;

(ii) Refers to 10 U.S.C. 2304(k) for armed services acquisitions or section 41 U.S.C. 3105 for civilian agency acquisitions; and

(iii) States that award to that entity shall be made in contravention of the merit-based selection procedures in 10 U.S.C. 2304(k) or 41 U.S.C. 3105, as appropriate. However, this limitation does not apply --

(A) When the work provided for in the contract is a continuation of the work performed by the specified entity under a preceding contract; or

(B) To any contract requiring the National Academy of Sciences to investigate, examine, or experiment upon any subject of science or art of significance to an executive agency and to report on those matters to the Congress or any agency of the Federal Government.

(2) Contracts awarded using this authority shall be supported by the written justifications and approvals described in 6.303 and 6.304, except for--

(i) Contracts awarded under (a)(2)(ii) or (b)(2) of this subsection;

(ii) Contracts awarded under (a)(2)(i) of this subsection when the statute expressly requires that the procurement be made from a specified source. (Justification and approval requirements apply when the statute authorizes, but does not require, that the procurement be made from a specified source); or

(iii) Contracts less than or equal to $22 million awarded under (b)(4) of this subsection.

(3) The authority in (a)(2)(ii) of this subsection may be used only for purchases of brand-name commercial items for resale through commissaries or other similar facilities. Ordinarily, these purchases will involve articles desired or preferred by customers of the selling activities when not providing for full and open competition, the contracting officer shall solicit offers from as many potential sources as is practicable under the circumstances.

FAR Subpart 6.302-6 -- National Security.

(a) *Authority.*

(1) Citations: 10 U.S.C. 2304(c)(6) or 41 U.S.C. 3304(a)(6).

(2) Full and open competition need not be provided for when the disclosure of the agency's needs would compromise the national security unless the agency is permitted to limit the number of sources from which it solicits bids or proposals.

(b) *Application.* This authority may be used for any acquisition when disclosure of the Government's needs would compromise the national security (*e.g.*, would violate security requirements); it shall not be used merely because the acquisition is classified, or merely because access to classified matter will be necessary to submit a proposal or to perform the contract.

(c) *Limitations.*

(1) Contracts awarded using this authority shall be supported by the written justifications and approvals described in 6.303 and 6.304.

(2) See 5.202(a)(1) for synopsis requirements, which is the synopsis cannot be worded to preclude disclosure of an agency's needs and such disclosure would compromise the national security (e.g., would result in disclosure of classified information). The fact that a proposed solicitation or contract action contains classified information, or that access to classified matter may be necessary to submit a proposal or perform the contract does not, in itself, justify use of this exception to synopsis.

(3) This statutory authority requires that agencies shall request offers from as many potential sources as is practicable under the circumstances.

FAR Subpart 6.302-7 -- Public Interest.

(a) *Authority.*

(1) Citations: 10 U.S.C. 2304(c)(7) or 41 U.S.C. 3304(a)(7).

(2) Full and open competition need not be provided for when the agency head determines that it is not in the public interest in the particular acquisition concerned.

(b) *Application.* This authority may be used when none of the other authorities in 6.302 apply.

(c) *Limitations.*

(1) A written determination to use this authority shall be made in accordance with Subpart 1.7, by --

(i) The Secretary of Defense, the Secretary of the Army, the Secretary of the Navy, the Secretary of the Air Force, the Secretary of Homeland Security for the Coast Guard, or the Administrator of the National Aeronautics and Space Administration; or

(ii) The head of any other executive agency. This authority may not be delegated.

(2) The Congress shall be notified in writing of such determination not less than 30 days before award of the contract.

(3) If required by the head of the agency, the contracting officer shall prepare a justification to support the determination under paragraph (c)(1) of this subsection.

(4) This Determination and Finding (D&F) shall not be made on a class basis.

FAR Subpart 13.106-1 Soliciting from a Single Source

In Accordance With FAR Subpart 13.106-1(b)(1)(i) For purchases not exceeding the simplified acquisition threshold ($250,000; may move to $700,000 if a declared disaster).

Contracting officers may solicit from one source if the contracting officer determines that the circumstances of the contract action deem only one source reasonably available (e.g., urgency, exclusive licensing agreements, and brand-name or industrial mobilization). The Justification shall be written just like the Justification an Approval in accordance with 6.303-2 (content; which will be outlined in Chapter 8 - Write it for the Contracting Officer!)

Supplemental Sole Sourcing

Each agency may have a supplement to the Federal Acquisition Regulation. Each Regulation may create stricter policy or may create more exceptions.

These are the following supplements:

1. Broadcasting Board of Governors
2. Defense Logistics Agency
3. Department of Agriculture Acquisition Regulation (AGAR)
4. Department of Commerce Acquisition Regulation (CAR)
5. Department of Defense Federal Acquisition Regulation Supplement (DFARS)
6. Department of Education Acquisition Regulation (EDAR)
7. Department of Energy Acquisition Regulation (DEAR)
8. Department of Health and Human Services Acquisition Regulation (HHSAR)
9. Department of Homeland Security Acquisition Regulation (HSAR)
10. Department of Housing and Urban Development Acquisition Regulation (HUDAR)
11. Department of Justice Acquisition Regulation (JAR)
12. Department of Labor Acquisition Regulation (DOLAR)
13. Department of State Acquisition Regulation (DOSAR)
14. Department of the Air Force Federal Acquisition Regulation Supplement (AFFARS)

15. Department of the Army Acquisition Regulations (AFARS)
16. Department of the Interior Acquisition Regulation (DIAR)
17. Department of the Navy Acquisition Regulations (NMCAR)
18. Department of the Treasury Acquisition Regulation (DTAR)
19. Department of Transportation Acquisition Regulation (TAR)
20. Department of Veterans Affairs Acquisition Regulation (VAAR)
21. Environmental Protection Agency Acquisition Regulation (EPAAR)
22. General Services Administration Acquisition Regulation (GSAR)
23. Office of Personnel Management Federal Employees' Life Insurance Federal Acquisition Regulation (LIFAR)
24. National Aeronautics and Space Administration Federal Acquisition Regulations Supplement (NASA)
25. National Science Foundation (NFS)
26. Nuclear Regulatory Commission Acquisition Regulation (NRCAR)
27. Office of Personnel Management Federal Employees Health Benefits Acquisition Regulation (FEHBAR)
28. Social Security Acquisition Regulation (SSAR)
29. U.S. Agency for International Development Acquisition Regulation (AIDAR)

The following agencies do not have an exception to sole source that supplements the Federal Acquisition Regulation that would be advantageous to the business trying to sell to the Government. There may be additional documentation, but does not provide an advantage to a business:

1. Defense Logistics Agency
2. Department of Housing and Urban Development Acquisition Regulation (HUDAR)
3. Department of Justice Acquisition Regulation (JAR)
4. Department of the Interior Acquisition Regulation (DIAR)
5. Department of the Navy Acquisition Regulations (NMCAR)
6. Department of the Treasury Acquisition Regulation (DTAR)
7. Department of Transportation Acquisition Regulation (TAR)
8. General Services Administration Acquisition Regulation (GSAR)
9. National Science Foundation (NFS)
10. Nuclear Regulatory Commission Acquisition Regulation (NRCAR)
11. Social Security Acquisition Regulation (SSAR)
12. U.S. Agency for International Development Acquisition Regulation (AIDAR)

The following agencies have an exception to sole source that supplements the Federal Acquisition Regulation that are advantageous to the business trying to sell to the Government:

1. Broadcasting Board of Governors
2. Department of Agriculture Acquisition Regulation (AGAR)
3. Department of Commerce Acquisition Regulation (CAR)
4. Department of Defense Federal Acquisition Regulation Supplement (DFARS)
5. Department of Education Acquisition Regulation (EDAR)
6. Department of Energy Acquisition Regulation (DEAR)
7. Department of Health and Human Services Acquisition Regulation (HHSAR)
8. Department of Homeland Security Acquisition Regulation (HSAR)
9. Department of Labor Acquisition Regulation (DOLAR)
10. Department of State Acquisition Regulation (DOSAR)
11. Department of the Air Force Federal Acquisition Regulation Supplement (AFFARS)
12. Department of the Army Acquisition Regulations (AFARS)
13. Department of Veterans Affairs Acquisition Regulation (VAAR)
14. Environmental Protection Agency Acquisition Regulation (EPAAR)
15. Life Insurance Federal Acquisition Regulation (LIFAR)
16. National Aeronautics and Space Administration Federal Acquisition Regulations Supplement (NASA)
17. Office of Personnel Management Federal Employees Health Benefits Acquisition Regulation (FEHBAR)

Broadcasting Board of Governors

The Broadcasting Board of Governors unique mission and the challenges associated with acquiring the unique services require through established federal procurement regulations, Congress has provided the USAGM with additional procurement authority that authorizes the agency to procure personal services through contracts [See 22 U.S.C. 6204(a)(15)(A)], and to conduct procurements without regard to any other provision of law relating to such procurements [See 22 U.S.C. 6204(a)(10)].

Where Congress has authorized a government entity to acquire goods or services "notwithstanding any other provision of law", those transactions, by their nature, are not subject to the Federal Acquisition Regulations (FAR), or to other procurement-related laws, such as the Competition in Contracting Act (CICA) [See 10 U.S.C. 2304, "…except in the case of procurement procedures otherwise expressly authorized by statute…"]

Notwithstanding these authorities, USAGM voluntarily follows the FAR in the conduct of most of its procurements, but reserves its right to exercise its authorities in those instances when competition poses severe challenges to the agency due to factors, such as geographical remoteness, uniqueness of requirement, requirements for unique skillsets, type of agreement, lack of public policy benefit, and other complexities related to the a fore listed.

Department of Agriculture Acquisition Regulation (AGAR)

AGAR 406.302-70 Otherwise authorized by law.

(a) <u>Authority.</u> Section 1472 of the National Agricultural Research, Extension, and Teaching Policy Act of 1977 (7 U.S.C. 3318) (the Act) authorizes the Secretary of Agriculture to award contracts, without competition, to further research, extension, or teaching programs in the food and agricultural sciences.

(b) <u>Limitations.</u> The use of this authority is limited to those instances where it can be determined that contracting without full and open competition is in the best interest of the Government and necessary to the accomplishment of the research, extension, or teaching program.

Therefore:

(1) Contracts under the authority of the Act shall be awarded on a competitive basis to the maximum practicable extent.

(2) When full and open competition is not deemed appropriate, the contracting officer shall make a written justification on a case-by-case basis in accordance with procedures in FAR 6.303 and 6.304.

Department of Commerce Acquisition Regulation (CAR)

CAR 1306.302-5 Authorized or required by statute.

In accordance with Executive Order 13457, a sole source acquisition may not be justified on the basis of any earmark included in any non-statutory source, except when otherwise required by law or when an earmark meets the criteria for funding set out in Executive Order 13457.

Executive Order 13457 of January 29, 2008

Protecting American Taxpayers from Government Spending on Wasteful Earmarks

By the authority vested in me as President by the Constitution and the laws of the United States of America, it is hereby ordered as follows:

Section 1. Policy. It is the policy of the Federal Government to be judicious in the expenditure of taxpayer dollars. To ensure the proper use of taxpayer funds that are appropriated for Government programs and purposes, it is necessary that the number and cost of earmarks be reduced, that their origin and purposes be transparent, and that they be included in the text of the bills voted upon by the Congress and presented to the President. For appropriations laws and other legislation enacted after the date of this order, executive agencies should not commit, obligate, or expend funds on the basis of earmarks included in any non-statutory source, including requests in reports of committees of the Congress or other congressional documents, or communications from or on behalf of Members of Congress, or any other non-statutory source, except when required by law or when an agency has itself determined a project, program, activity, grant, or other transaction to have merit under statutory criteria or other merit-based decision-making.

Sec. 2. Duties of Agency Heads.

(a) With respect to all appropriations laws and other legislation enacted after the date of this order, the head of each agency shall take all necessary steps to ensure that:

(i) agency decisions to commit, obligate, or expend funds for any earmark are based on the text of laws, and in particular, are not based on language in any report of a committee of Congress, joint explanatory statement of a committee of conference of the Congress, statement of managers concerning a bill in the Congress, or any other non-statutory statement or indication of views of the Congress, or a House, committee, Member, officer, or staff thereof;

(ii) agency decisions to commit, obligate, or expend funds for any earmark are based on authorized, transparent, statutory criteria and merit-based decision making, in the manner set forth in section II of OMB Memorandum M–07–10, dated February 15, 2007, to the extent consistent with applicable law; and

(iii) No oral or written communications concerning earmarks shall supersede statutory criteria, competitive awards, or merit-based decision-making.

(b) An agency shall not consider the views of a House, committee, Member, officer, or staff of the Congress with respect to commitments, obligations, or expenditures to carry out any earmark unless such views are in writing, to facilitate consideration in accordance with section 2(a)(ii) above. All written communications from the Congress, or a House, committee, Member, officer, or staff thereof, recommending that funds be committed, obligated, or expended on any earmark shall be made publicly available on the Internet by the receiving agency, not later than 30 days after receipt of such communication, unless otherwise specifically directed by the head of the agency, without delegation, after consultation with the Director of the Office of Management and Budget, to preserve appropriate confidentiality between the executive and legislative branches.

(c) Heads of agencies shall otherwise implement within their respective agencies the policy set forth in section 1 of this order, consistent with such instructions as the Director of the Office of Management and Budget may prescribe.

(d) The head of each agency shall upon request provide to the Director of the Office of Management and Budget information about earmarks and compliance with this order.

Sec. 3. Definitions. For purposes of this order:

(a) The term ''agency'' means an executive agency as defined in section 105 of title 5, United States Code, and the United States Postal Service and the Postal Regulatory Commission, but shall exclude the Government Accountability Office; and

(b) the term ''earmark'' means funds provided by the Congress for projects, programs, or grants where the purported congressional direction (whether in statutory text, report language, or other communication) circumvents otherwise applicable merit-based or competitive allocation processes, or specifies the location or recipient, or otherwise curtails the ability of the executive branch to manage its statutory and constitutional responsibilities pertaining to the fund's allocation process.

Sec. 4. General Provisions.

(a) Nothing in this order shall be construed to impair or otherwise affect:

    (i) Authority granted by law to an agency or the head thereof; or

    (ii) Functions of the Director of the Office of Management and Budget relating to budget, administrative, or legislative proposals.

(b) This order shall be implemented in a manner consistent with applicable law and subject to the availability of appropriations.

(c) This order is not intended to, and does not, create any right or benefit, substantive or procedural, enforceable at law or in equity, by any party against the United States, its agencies, instrumentalities, or entities, its officers, employees, or agents, or any other person.

Reference: https://www.govinfo.gov/content/pkg/FR-2008-02-01/pdf/08-483.pdf

Department of Defense Federal Acquisition Regulation Supplement (DFARS)

** The information in the DFARS Section is information for approval processes or additional information that may be needed for the Justification and Approval.

206.302-1 Only one responsible source and no other supplies or services will satisfy agency requirements.

   (a) Authority.

   (2)(i) Section 8059 of Pub. L. 101-511 and similar sections in subsequent defense appropriations acts, prohibit departments and agencies from entering into contracts for studies, analyses, or consulting services (see FAR Subpart 37.2) on the basis of an unsolicited proposal without providing for full and open competition, unless—

   (1) The head of the contracting activity, or a designee no lower than chief of the contracting office, determines that—

   (i)   Following thorough technical evaluation, only one source is fully qualified to perform the proposed work;

   (ii) The unsolicited proposal offers significant scientific or technological promise, represents the product of original thinking, and was submitted in confidence; or

   (iii) The contract benefits the national defense by taking advantage of a unique and significant industrial accomplishment or by ensuring financial support to a new product or idea;

(2) A civilian official of the DOD, whose appointment has been confirmed by the Senate, determines the award to be in the interest of national defense; or

(3) The contract is related to improvement of equipment that is in development or production.

(b) Application. This authority may be used for acquisitions of test articles and associated support services from a designated foreign source under the DoD Foreign Comparative Testing Program.

(d) Limitations. Follow the procedures at PGI 206.302-1(d) prior to soliciting a proposal without providing for full and open competition under this authority.

PGI 206.302-1 Only one responsible source and no other supplies or services will satisfy agency requirements.

(d) Limitations. When utilizing the authority at FAR 6.302-1, the contracting officer shall post a request for information or a sources sought notice, and shall include the results of this inquiry in the justification required by FAR 6.303. This requirement to post may be waived by the Head of the Contracting Activity, or designee. The waiver authority may not be delegated lower than a general or flag officer or a member of the Senior Executive Service.

206.302-2 Unusual and compelling urgency.

(b) *Application*. For guidance on circumstances under which use of this authority may be appropriate, see PGI 206.302-2(b).

PGI 206.302-2 Unusual and compelling urgency.

(b) *Application.* The circumstances under which use of this authority may be appropriate include, but are not limited to, the following:

(i) Supplies, services, or construction needed at once because of fire, flood, explosion, or other disaster.

(ii) Essential equipment or repair needed at once to-

    (A) Comply with orders for a ship;

    (B) Perform the operational mission of an aircraft; or

    (C) Preclude impairment of launch capabilities or mission performance of missiles or missile support equipment.

(iii) Construction needed at once to preserve a structure or its contents from damage.

(iv) Purchase requests citing an issue priority designator under DoD Manual 4140.01, Volume 5, DoD Supply Chain Materiel Management Procedures: Delivery of Material, of 4 or higher, or citing "Electronic Warfare QRC Priority."

206.302-4 International agreement.

(c) *Limitations.* Pursuant to 10 U.S.C. 2304(f)(2)(E), the justifications and approvals described in FAR 6.303 and 6.304 are not required if the head of the contracting activity prepares a document that describes the terms of an agreement or treaty or the written directions, such as a Letter of Offer and Acceptance, that have the effect of requiring the use of other than competitive procedures for the acquisition.

206.302-5 Authorized or required by statute.

(b) *Application.* Agencies may use this authority to—

(i) Acquire supplies and services from military exchange stores outside the United States for use by the armed forces outside the United States in accordance with 10 U.S.C. 2424(a) and subject to the limitations of 10 U.S.C. 2424(b). The limitations of 10 U.S.C. 2424(b)(1) and (2) do not apply to the purchase of soft drinks that are manufactured in the United States. For the purposes of 10 U.S.C. 2424, soft drinks manufactured in the United States are brand name carbonated sodas, manufactured in the United States, as evidenced by product markings.

(ii) Acquire police, fire protection, airfield operation, or other community services from local governments at military installations to be closed under the circumstances in 237.7401 (Section 2907 of Fiscal Year 1994 Defense Authorization Act (Pub. L. 103-160)).

(c) *Limitations*.

(i) 10 U.S.C. 2361 precludes use of this exception for awards to colleges or universities for the performance of research and development, or for the construction of any research or other facility, unless—

(A) The statute authorizing or requiring award specifically—

(1) States that the statute modifies or supersedes the provisions of 10 U.S.C. 2361,

(2) Identifies the particular college or university involved, and

(3) States that award is being made in contravention of 10 U.S.C. 2361(a); and

(B) The Secretary of Defense provides Congress written notice of intent to award. The contract cannot be awarded until 180 days have elapsed since the date Congress received the notice of intent to award.

Contracting activities must submit a draft notice of intent with supporting documentation through channels to the Director of Defense Procurement and Acquisition Policy, Office of the Under Secretary of Defense (Acquisition, Technology, and Logistics).

(ii) The limitation in paragraph (c)(i) of this subsection applies only if the statute authorizing or requiring award was enacted after September 30, 1989.

(iii) Subsequent statutes may provide different or additional constraints on the award of contracts to specified colleges and universities. Contracting officers should consult legal counsel on a case-by-case basis.

206.302-7 Public interest.

(c) *Limitations.* For the defense agencies, the written determination to use this authority must be made by the Secretary of Defense.

213.500-70 Only one offer.

If only one offer is received in response to a competitive solicitation issued using simplified acquisition procedures authorized under FAR subpart 13.5, follow the procedures at 215.371-2.

215.371-2 Promote competition.

Except as provided in sections 215.371-4 (See further down) and 215.371-5—

(a) If only one offer is received when competitive procedures were used and the (See further down) solicitation allowed fewer than 30 days for receipt of proposals, the contracting officer shall—

(1) Consult with the requiring activity as to whether the requirements document should be revised in order to promote more competition (see FAR 6.502(b)

Agency advocates for competition and 11.002 Policy – needs for market research); and

(2) Resolicit, allowing an additional period of at least 30 days for receipt of proposals; and

(b) For competitive solicitations in which more than one potential offeror expressed an interest in an acquisition, but only one offer was ultimately received, follow the procedures at PGI 215.371-2 (DFARS/PGI view).

PGI 215.371-2 Promote competition – DFARS/PGI view.

(a) For competitive solicitations in which more than one potential offeror expressed an interest in an acquisition, but only one offer was ultimately received, the Contracting Officer shall—

(1) Seek feedback (e.g., issue an RFI) after award from potential offerors expected to submit an offer; and

(2) Document any feedback received in the contract file.

(b) Agencies shall use any feedback received when considering how to overcome barriers to competition for future requirements

215.371-4 Exceptions.

(a) The requirements at sections 215.371-2 (Promote competition) do not apply to—

(1) Acquisitions at or below the simplified acquisition threshold;

(2) Acquisitions, as determined by the head of the contracting activity, in support of contingency or humanitarian or peacekeeping operations; to facilitate defense against or recovery from cyber, nuclear, biological, chemical, or radiological attack; to facilitate the

provision of international disaster assistance; or to support response to an emergency or major disaster;

(3) Small business set-asides under FAR subpart 19.5, set asides offered and accepted into the 8(a) Program under FAR subpart 19.8, or set-asides under the HUBZone Program (see FAR 19.1305(c)), the Service-Disabled Veteran-Owned Small Business Procurement Program (see FAR 19.1405(c)), or the Women-Owned Small Business Program (see FAR 19.1505(d));

(4) Acquisitions of basic or applied research or development, as specified in FAR 35.016(a), that use a broad agency announcement; or

(5) Acquisitions of architect-engineer services (see FAR 36.601-2).

(b) The applicability of an exception in paragraph (a) of this section does not eliminate the need for the contracting officer to seek maximum practicable competition and to ensure that the price is fair and reasonable.

213.501 Special documentation requirements.

(a) *Sole source (including brand name) acquisitions.* For Noncompetitive follow-on acquisitions of supplies or services previously awarded on a Noncompetitive basis, include the additional documentation required by 206.303-2(b)(i) and follow the procedures at PGI 206.304(a)(S-70).

206.303-2(b)(i)

(b)(i) Include the information required by PGI 206.303-2(b)(i) (DFARS/PGI view) in justifications citing the authority at FAR 6.302 (Circumstances Permitting Other Than Full and Open Competition.)

PGI 206.303-2(b)(i) –

(b)(i) Justifications citing the authority at FAR 6.302-1 to permit the use of other than full and open competition, shall—

(A) Include the results of the request for information or sources sought notice posted in accordance with PGI 206.302-1 (unless the requirement to post has been waived); and

(B) For Noncompetitive follow-on acquisitions of supplies or services previously awarded on a Noncompetitive basis, include a copy of the previous justification to assist the approval authority in determining whether the planned actions to remove any barriers to competition cited on the previous justification were completed.

PGI 206.304(a)(S-70)

PGI 206.304 Approval of the justification.

(a)(S-70) For a Noncompetitive follow-on to a previous award for the same supply or service supported by a justification for other than full and open competition citing the authority at FAR 6.302-1—

(i) The justification shall include a copy of the previous justification to assist the approval authority in determining whether the planned actions to remove any barriers to competition cited on the previous justification were completed; and

(ii) The approval authority shall determine whether the planned actions were completed. If the actions were not completed, the justification for the follow-on acquisition shall be approved by the approval authority one-level above the approval authority for the previous justification (see FAR 6.304). If the previous justification was approved by the Senior Procurement Executive (SPE), the approval remains at the SPE level.

Department of Education Acquisition Regulation (EDAR)

3406.302-5 Authorized or required by statute.

    (a) *Authority.*

        (1) Citations: 20 U.S.C. 1018a.

        (2) Noncompetitive awards of successive modules for systems are permitted when the conditions set forth in 3417.70 are met.

3417.70 Modular contracting.

    (a) FSA—May incrementally conduct successive procurements of modules of overall systems. Each module must be useful in its own right or useful in combination with the earlier procurement modules. Successive modules may be procured on a sole source basis under the following circumstances:

        (1) Competitive procedures are used for awarding the contract for the first system module; and

        (2) The solicitation for the first module included the following:

            (i) A general description of the entire system that was sufficient to provide potential offerors with reasonable notice of the general scope of future modules;

            (ii) Other sufficient information to enable offerors to make informed business decisions to submit offers for the first module; and

            (iii) A statement that procedures, i.e., the sole source awarding of follow-on modules, could be used for the subsequent awards.

Department of Energy Acquisition Regulation (DEAR)

Subpart 906.3 — Other Than Full and Open Competition

906.304 Approval of the justification.

(c) Class justifications within the delegated authority of a Head of the Contracting Activity may be approved for:

(1) Contracts for electric power or energy, gas (natural or manufactured), water, or other utility services when such services are available from only one source;

(2) Contracts under the authority cited in FAR 6.302-4 or 6.302-5; or

(3) Contracts for educational services from nonprofit institutions. Class justifications for classes of actions that may exceed $10,000,000 require the approval of the Senior Procurement Executive.

Department of Health and Human Services Acquisition Regulation (HHSAR)

306.302-1 Only one responsible source and no other supplies or services will satisfy agency requirements. See FAR 6.302-1.

For acquisitions covered by 42 U.S.C. 247d-6a(b)(2)(A), "available from only one responsible source" shall be deemed to mean "available from only one responsible source or only from a limited number of responsible sources".

(A) Qualified countermeasure The term "qualified countermeasure" means a drug (as that term is defined by section 321(g)(1) of title 21), biological product (as that term is defined by section 262(i) of this title), or device (as that term is defined by section 321(h) of title 21), that the Secretary determines to be a priority (consistent with sections 182(2) and 184(a) of title 6)—

  (i) to diagnose, mitigate, prevent, or treat harm from any biological agent (including organisms that cause an infectious disease) or toxin, chemical, radiological, or nuclear agent that may cause a public health emergency affecting national security;

  (ii) to diagnose, mitigate, prevent, or treat harm from a condition that may result in adverse health consequences or death and may be caused by administering a drug, biological product, or device that is used as described in this subparagraph; or

  (iii) is a product or technology intended to enhance the use or effect of a drug, biological product, or device described in clause (i) or (ii).

Department of Homeland Security Acquisition Regulation (HSAR)

3006.302-1 Only one responsible source and no other supplies or services will satisfy agency requirements.

(b)(4) The contracting officer may rely on this exception in the case where only one source is available to provide additional units or replacement items under a specific make and model requirement, but only where the CPO has determined in accordance with the agency's standardization program that only the specific make(s) and model(s) will satisfy the agency's needs.

3006.302-270 Unusual and compelling urgency.

(d)(1)(iii) For contract awards to facilitate the response to or recovery from a natural disaster, act of terrorism, or other man-made disaster, that relies on this exception, <u>the period of performance shall be limited to the minimum period necessary to meet the urgent and compelling requirements of the work to be performed and to enter into another contract for the required goods or services through the use of competitive procedures, but in no event shall the period of performance exceed 150 days</u>, unless the Head of the Contracting Activity (or higher approval authority if required by (FAR) 48 CFR 6.304 or DHS procedures) determines that exceptional circumstances apply, approving the justification as set forth in (HSAR) 48 CFR 3006.304. The limitation on the period of performance applies to contracts awarded in response to, or to recovery from:

   (A) A major disaster or emergency declared by the President under Title IV or Title V of the Robert T. Stafford Disaster Relief and Emergency Assistance Act, as amended (42 U.S.C. 5121-5207) (see http://www.fema.gov/news/disasters.fema#sev2 for a list of declarations);

(B) An uncontrolled fire or fire complex, threatening such destruction as would constitute a major disaster, and for which the Federal Emergency Management Agency has approved a fire management assistance declaration in accordance with regulatory criteria at 44 CFR 204.21 (see http://www.fema.gov/news/disasters.fema#sev2 for a list of declarations);

(C) An incident for which the National Operations Center (NOC), through the National Response Coordination Center (NRCC), coordinates the activation of the appropriate Emergency Support Functions and the Secretary of Homeland Security has designated a Federal Resource Coordinator (FRC) to manage Federal resource support.

3006.302-7 Public interest.

(c)(1)(ii) Requests shall be prepared in writing by the contracting officer, using the format found in (HSAR) 48 CFR 3001.704, and submitted through the HCA to the CPO for review and transmittal to the Secretary for approval.

3006.303 Justifications.

3006.303-270 Content.

(a)(9)(iv) For a proposed contract subject to the restrictions of (HSAR) 48 CFR 3006.302-270(d)(1)(iii)and where (FAR) 48 CFR 6.302-2 is cited as the authority, the exceptional circumstances allowing for an award for a period of performance in excess of 150 days.

3006.304 Approval of justification.

3006.304-70 DHS Approval of justification.

A justification for other than full and open competition that cites (FAR) 48 CFR Part 6.302-2 as its authority shall be approved in writing by the HCA (unless a higher approval authority is required in accordance with (FAR) 48 CFR Part 6.304 or DHS procedures) for a proposed DHS contract to facilitate the response to or recovery from a natural disaster, act of terrorism, or other man-made disaster with a period of performance in excess of 150 days. The justification should make plain the exceptional circumstances that justify the duration of the contract. This authority may not be redelegated by the HCA.

Hint

1. FEMA is allowed to sole source for 150 days, then has to compete the contract within the declared disaster counties. The only exception to get outside of the local area set-aside is if the Contacting Officer does a determination and finding that determines that a local area set-aside (declared county businesses) are unable to provide the supply, or perform the construction or service. ONLY THE COUNTIES SHOULD BE COMPETING THAT ARE DECLARED WITHIN THE DISASTER. Contracts can be longer if the Head of the Contracting Activity (or higher approval authority if required by (FAR) 48 CFR 6.304 or DHS procedures) determines that exceptional circumstances apply.

2. To look at disasters go to https://www.fema.gov/disasters#sev2. Click on the disaster and you are able to see which counties are declared.

3. Review Chapter 2 - Market Research – Historical Contract to determine which NAICS Codes are used per disaster.

4. The following FAR Clauses shall be in the contract and list the counties. If the counties are not listed. As a company place your quote, bid, or proposal. Some Contracting Officer will put the disaster number. That is not the standard if you read what the clauses state.

READ THE PROVISION AND CLAUSES

See the following clauses:

52.226-3 – Disaster or Emergency Area Representation (Nov 2007)

(a) Set-aside area. The area covered in this contract is: _____
[Contracting Officer to fill in with definite geographic boundaries.]

(b) Representations. The offeror represents that it [ ] does [ ] does not reside or primarily do business in the set-aside area.

(c) An offeror is considered to be residing or primarily doing business in the set-aside area if, during the last twelve months—

(1) The offeror had its main operating office in the area; and

(2) That office generated at least half of the offeror's gross revenues and employed at least half of the offeror's permanent employees.

(d) If the offeror does not meet the criteria in paragraph (c) of this provision, factors to be considered in determining whether an offeror resides or primarily does business in the set-aside area include—

(1) Physical location(s) of the offeror's permanent office(s) and date any office in the set-aside area(s) was established;

(2) Current state licenses;

(3) Record of past work in the set-aside area(s) (*e.g.,* how much and for how long);

(4) Contractual history the offeror has had with subcontractors and/or suppliers in the set-aside area;

(5) Percentage of the offeror's gross revenues attributable to work performed in the set-aside area;

(6) Number of permanent employees the offeror employs in the set-aside area;

(7) Membership in local and state organizations in the set-aside area; and

(8) Other evidence that establishes the offeror resides or primarily does business in the set-aside area. For example, sole proprietorships may submit utility bills and bank statements.

(e) If the offeror represents it resides or primarily does business in the set-aside area, the offeror shall furnish documentation to support its representation if requested by the Contracting Officer. The solicitation may require the offeror to submit with its offer documentation to support the representation.

(End of provision)

52.226-4 – Notice of Disaster or Emergency Area Set-Aside (Nov 2007)

(a) Set-aside area. Offers are solicited only from businesses residing or primarily doing business in _____ [*Contracting Officer to fill in with definite geographic boundaries.*] Offers received from other businesses shall not be considered.

(b) This set-aside is in addition to any small business set-aside contained in this contract.

(End of provision)

52.226-5 – Restrictions on Subcontracting Outside Disaster or Emergency Area (Nov 2007)

(a) *Definitions.* The definitions of the following terms used in this clause are found in the Small Business Administration regulations at 13 CFR 125.6(e): cost of the contract, cost of contract performance incurred for personnel, cost of manufacturing, cost of materials, personnel, and subcontracting.

(b) The Contractor agrees that in performance of the contract in the case of a contract for—

(1) Services (except construction). At least 50 percent of the cost of contract performance incurred for personnel shall be expended for employees of the Contractor or employees of other businesses residing or primarily doing business in the clause at FAR 52.226-4, Notice of Disaster or Emergency Area Set-Aside;

(2) Supplies (other than procurement from a nonmanufacturer of such supplies). The Contractor or employees of other businesses residing or primarily doing business in the set-aside area shall perform work for at least 50 percent of the cost of manufacturing the supplies, not including the cost of materials;

(3) General construction. The Contractor will perform at least 15 percent of the cost of the contract, not including the cost of materials, with its own employees or employees of other businesses residing or primarily doing business in the set-aside area; or

(4) Construction by special trade Contractors. The Contractor will perform at least 25 percent of the cost of the contract, not including the cost of materials, with its own employees or employees of other businesses residing or primarily doing business in the set-aside area.   (End of clause)

Department of Labor Acquisition Regulation (DOLAR)

2906.301 Policy.

(a) Department of Labor acquisitions must comply with the Department of Labor Manual Series (DLMS) 2, Chapter 830 (available by mail from the Director, Division of Acquisition Management Services, 200 Constitution Ave., NW., Washington, DC 20210-0001), or electronically from https://www.dol.gov/oasam/boc/oams/prb.htm. Any proposed noncompetitive acquisition in excess of the simplified acquisition threshold must be fully justified and, if required by the DLMS, submitted to the DOL Procurement Review Board and approved by the Assistant Secretary for Administration and Management and, in the case of research and development contracts, also by the Assistant Secretary for Policy.

(b) With the exception of contracts for advisory and assistance services or for research and development, the contracting officer has the authority below the simplified acquisition threshold to approve sole source contracts. The contracting officer is responsible for assuring that proposed acquisitions below the simplified acquisition threshold are in compliance with FAR and DOLAR requirements regarding competition.

Department of State Acquisition Regulation (DOSAR)

606.302-4 International agreement.

    (b)(2) In accordance with FAR 6.302-4, guard services shall be acquired from the host Government only when it is the sole available source.

606.302-6 National security.

(b) This subsection applies to all acquisitions involving national security information, regardless of dollar amount. In no case shall information be classified in order to restrict competition. Information may be classified only when its authorized disclosure could be expected to cause damage to national security.

(c)(1) The Chief, Controls Division, Office of Intelligence Liaison, Directorate for Coordination, Bureau of Intelligence and Research is responsible for reviewing and certifying on any proposed acquisitions derived from or funded or administered by intelligence community agencies that involve sensitive compartmented information and ensuring that the provisions of Executive Order 13526 and FAR 6.302-6 have been met. The Office Director, Office of Information Security, Security Infrastructure Directorate, Bureau of Diplomatic Security (DS/SI/IS), is responsible for reviewing and certifying on all other proposed acquisitions funded by the Department of State that involve national security information and ensuring that the provisions of Executive Order 13526 and FAR 6.302-6 have been met. When disclosure of the Department's needs through full and open competition would compromise national security, the Justification for Other than Full and Open Competition shall include the following specific information:

    (i) How national security would be compromised if the Department of State's (or other agencies') needs were disclosed in the GPE;

(ii) Why the GPE notice cannot be worded in such a manner that national security would not be compromised;

(iii) Necessity for access to classified information to prepare technical and/or cost proposal and level of security clearance required;

(iv) Necessity for access to classified information to perform the proposed contract and level of security clearance required;

(v) Number and value of contracts that the justification covers; and

(vi) A statement as follows: "I hereby certify that the national security concerns of the referenced acquisition(s) meet the criteria set forth in Executive Order 12958 and FAR 6.302-6."

(2) Any acquisition involving national security information shall be publicized in the GPE unless disclosure of the agency's needs would compromise national security.

(3) The contracting officer is responsible for soliciting offers from as many potential sources as is practicable under the circumstances. However, given the sensitivity required for acquisitions involving national security information, it is expected that requirements offices will work closely with the contracting officer in maximizing competition.

606.370 Department of State standardization program.

(a) It is the Department's policy to promote full and open competition in all procurement actions. The authority at 41 U.S.C. 3304(a)(1) shall be used with respect to standardization when only specified makes and models of equipment will satisfy the Department's needs and only one source is available. This policy applies to all acquisitions involving standardization, regardless of dollar amount.

Department of the Air Force Federal Acquisition Regulation Supplement (AFFARS)

** The information in the AFFARS Section is information for approval processes or additional information that may be needed for the Justification and Approval.

5306.302-1 Only One Responsible Source and No Other Supplies or Services Will Satisfy Agency Requirements

(a)(2)(i)*(1)* See MP5301.601(a)(i).

(d) See MP5301.601(a)(i).

See http://farsite.hill.af.mil/reghtml/regs/far2afmcfars/af_afmc/affars/MP5301.601(a)(i).htm

306.302-2 Unusual and Compelling Urgency

(c)(1) Contracting Officers must notify SAF/AQC and their MAJCOM/DRU/AFRCO SCO (or for AFLCMC and SMC, the SCCO) as soon as practicable when contemplating the use of this authority for a J&A requiring Senior Procurement Executive (SPE) approval.

(d)(1)(ii) The DAS(C) and the ADAS(C) are the authority to make this determination for the Air Force. This authority is not further delegated.

5306.302-4 International Agreement

(c) *Limitations.* The document referred to in DFARS 206.302-4(c) must be titled, "*International Agreement Competitive Restrictions (IACR).*" The authority to prepare an IACR is delegated from the HCA to the contracting officer (see MP5301.601(a)(i)). The contracting officer must include the IACR and a copy of the associated *Letter of Offer and Acceptance*, once completed, in the contract file.

5313.501 Special Documentation Requirements

(a)(1)(ii) Contracting officers must cite the applicable statutory authority permitting other than full and open competition as established in 10 U.S.C. 2302b, Implementation of Simplified Acquisition Procedures (41 U.S.C. 1901), or 10 U.S.C 2304(a), Special Emergency Procurement Authority (41 U.S.C. 1903). For sole source acquisitions using simplified acquisition procedures that exceed the simplified acquisition threshold but do not exceed $7M ($13M for acquisitions described in FAR 13.500(c)), the tailorable Sole Source (Including Brand Name) Justification - Simplified Procedures for Certain Commercial Items template may be used.

(a)(2) See 5306.304(a) for the approving officials for acquisitions using the limited or sole source justification at FAR 13.501(a)(2).

5306.304 Approval of the Justification

(a)

Justification Value	Approval Authority	Delegability
≤ $700K	Chief of the Contracting Office	Delegable to Contracting Officer, consistent with warrant level
> $700K ≤ $13.5M	Procuring Activity Competition Advocate	Not further delegable
> $13.5M ≤ $93M	PEO / Head of Procuring Activity / Designated Alternate if they meet the criteria in FAR 6.304(a)(3). If they do not meet the criteria in FAR 6.304(a)(3) = Senior Procurement Executive	Delegable to Flag / General Officer or civilian SES
> $93M*	Senior Procurement Executive	Not further delegable

Department of the Army Acquisition Regulations (AFARS)

** The information in the AFARS Section is information for approval processes or additional

information that may be needed for the Justification and Approval.

5106.302-1 Only one responsible source and no other supplies or services will satisfy agency requirements.

(a)(2)(i)(1) The head of the contracting activity shall make the determination at DFARS 206.302-1(a)(2)(i)(1). See Appendix GG for further delegation.
http://farsite.hill.af.mil/reghtml/regs/other/afars/GG_27_01.htm

(d) The head of the contracting activity may waive the requirements as stated in DFARS and DFARS PGI 206.302-1(d). See Appendix GG for further delegation.
http://farsite.hill.af.mil/reghtml/regs/other/afars/GG_27_01.htm

5106.302-2 Unusual and compelling urgency.

(d)(1)(ii) The Assistant Secretary of the Army (Acquisition, Logistics and Technology) shall make the determination that exceptional circumstances apply as described in FAR 6.302-2(d)(1)(ii) - May not exceed one year, including all options, unless the head of the agency determines that exceptional circumstances apply. This determination must be documented in the contract file. See Appendix GG for further delegation.
http://farsite.hill.af.mil/reghtml/regs/other/afars/GG_27_01.htm

(2)(ii) The Assistant Secretary of the Army (Acquisition, Logistics and Technology) shall make the determination for any subsequent modification as set forth in FAR 6.302-2(d)(2)(ii). See Appendix GG for further delegation.
http://farsite.hill.af.mil/reghtml/regs/other/afars/GG_27_01.htm

5106.302-3 Industrial mobilization; engineering, developmental, or research capability; or expert services.

(c) *Limitations.* When citing the authority at 10 U.S.C. 2304(c)(3) as implemented in FAR 6.302-3(a)(2)(ii), the contracting officer must ensure the certifications required by FAR 6.303-1(c) and FAR 6.303-2(c) contain a statement that the technical and requirements personnel reviewed the proposed effort to ensure that it falls within the charter or special capabilities of the proposed institution. In addition, the statement will explain how the proposed effort establishes or maintains (as appropriate) an essential engineering, research, or development capability to be provided by an educational or other non-profit institution or a federally funded research and development center (FFRDC). When proposing to contract directly with an FFRDC not sponsored by the contracting activity, the contracting officer must ensure that the procurement request includes a written confirmation from the sponsoring agency that the proposed effort falls within the mission and general scope of effort or special competency of the FFRDC.

5106.302-4 International agreement.

(c) *Limitations.* When citing the authority at 10 U.S.C. 2304(c)(4) as implemented in FAR 6.302-4 and DFARS 206.302-4(c), the contracting officer must ensure the document referred to in DFARS 206.302-4(c) is titled "International Agreement Competitive Restrictions" (IACR). The IACR describes the terms of an international agreement or treaty, or the written directions of a foreign government reimbursing the cost of the procurement, that have the effect of requiring other than competitive procedures for the procurement. The IACR may be used even when the terms of the agreement or treaty, or the written directions, do not specifically name a required source, provided the agreement or treaty, or the written directions, contain sufficient information to explain why the use of other than competitive procedures is required. The HCA may delegate authority to prepare an IACR to a level no lower than the chief of the contracting office. The contracting officer must include in the contract file the IACR and a copy of the associated Letter of Offer and Acceptance, or other international agreement, treaty, or written directions of the reimbursing foreign government.

Department of Veterans Affairs Acquisition Regulation (VAAR)

806.302-5-70 Noncompetitive procedures for verified small business concerns owned and controlled by Veterans.

(a) Full and open competition need not be provided for when awarding a sole source contract with a verified SDVOSB or a verified VOSB in accordance with 819.7007 or 819.7008 as authorized. Pursuant to FAR 6.302-5(c)(2)(ii) (Contracts awarded under (a)(2)(i) of this subsection when the statute expressly requires that the procurement be made from a specified source. (Justification and approval requirements apply when the statute authorizes, but does not require, that the procurement be made from a specified source)), the justification and approval requirements of FAR 6.303 and 6.304 apply.

(b) Noncompetitive procedures for contracts below the Simplified Acquisition Threshold. When entering into a contract with a verified small business concern owned and controlled by veterans for an amount less than the simplified acquisition threshold, a contracting officer may use procedures other than competitive procedures. (Cite: 41 U.S.C. 3304(a)(5), as authorized by 38 U.S.C. 8127(b)).

(c) Sole source contracts above the Simplified Acquisition Threshold. (Cite: 41 U.S.C. 3304(a)(5), as authorized by 38 U.S.C. 8127(c)). A contracting officer may award a contract to a verified small business concern owned and controlled by Veterans using procedures other than competitive procedures if—

   (1) The anticipated award price of the contract (including options) will exceed the simplified acquisition threshold, but will not exceed $5 million; and

   (2) In the estimation of the contracting officer, the contract award can be made at a fair and reasonable price that offers best value to the United States.

VAAR 819.7007 or 819.7008

(a) A contracting officer may award a contract to a verified VOSB or SDVOSB concern using procedures other than competitive procedures provided–

   (1) The anticipated award price of the contract (including options) will not exceed $5 million;

   (2) The justification prepared pursuant to FAR 6.302-5(c)(2)(ii) is posted in accordance with FAR subpart 5.301(d) ;

   (3) The VOSB or SDVOSB concern has been determined to be a responsible source with respect to performance; and

   (4) In the estimation of the contracting officer, contract award can be made at a fair and reasonable price that offers best value to the Government.

(b) The contracting officer's determination to make a sole source award is a business decision wholly within the discretion of the contracting officer. To ensure that opportunities are available to the broadest number of verified VOSBs or SDVOSBs, this authority is to be used judiciously and only when in the best interest of the Government.

Environmental Protection Agency Acquisition Regulation (EPAAR)

1506.302-5 Authorized or required by statute.

(a) *Authority.* Section 109(e) of the Superfund Amendments and Reauthorization Act of 1986 (SARA) is cited as authority.

(b) *Application.* (1) The contracting officer may use other than full and open competition to acquire the services of experts for use in preparing or prosecuting a civil or criminal action under SARA whether or not the expert is expected to testify at trial. The contracting officer need not prepare the written justification under FAR 6.303 when acquiring expert services under the authority of section 109(e) of SARA. The contracting officer shall document the official contract file when using this authority.

(2) The contracting officer shall give notice to the Agency's Competition Advocate whenever a contract award is made using other than full and open competition under this authority. The notice shall contain a copy of the contract and the summary of negotiations.

The Superfund Amendments and Reauthorization Act (SARA) 109(e)

109 (e) PROCUREMENT PROCEDURES.—Notwithstanding any other provision of law, any executive agency may use competitive procedures or procedures other than competitive procedures to procure the services of experts for use in preparing or prosecuting a civil or criminal action under this Act, whether or not the expert is expected to testify at trial. The executive agency need not provide any written justification for the use of procedures other than competitive procedures when procuring such expert services under this Act and need not furnish for publication in the Commerce Business Daily or otherwise any notice of solicitation or synopsis with respect to such procurement.

Office of Personnel Management Federal Employees' Life Insurance Federal Acquisition Regulation (LIFAR)

2106.7001 Applicability.

FAR part 6 has no practical application to the FEGLI Program because 5 U.S.C. chapter 87 exempts the FEGLI Program from competitive bidding.

National Aeronautics and Space Administration Federal Acquisition Regulations Supplement (NASA)

1806.302-4 International agreement.

(c) Pursuant to 10 U.S.C. 2304(f)(2)(E), an individual justification for other than full and open competition under the authority of FAR 6.302-4 is not required when the procurement officer signs a Memorandum for the Record that describes the specific terms of the international agreement or treaty that limit acquisitions in support of, or as a result of, the agreement or treaty to less than full and open competition.

1806.302-7 Public interest.

(c)(2) The NASA Headquarters, Office of Legislative and Intergovernmental Affairs is responsible for notifying Congress. The Office of Procurement, Program Operations Division shall request the notice to Congress be made immediately upon approval of a D&F and shall advise the contracting activity of the date upon which the notification period ends.

(3) The contracting officer shall prepare the D&F required by FAR 6.302-7(c)(1) in any format that clearly documents the determination and the supporting findings.

1806.303-1 Requirements.

(c) Justifications for using less than full and open competition may be prepared by the technical office initiating the contract action when it is recommending the use of the justification authority, or by the contracting officer if the technical office does not make such a recommendation.

(d) The contracting officer shall send a copy of each approved justification or D&F that cites the authority of FAR 6.302-7 to NASA Headquarters, Office of Procurement, Program Operations Division, unless one of the exceptions at FAR 25.401 applies to the acquisition. The transmittal shall indicate that the justification is being furnished under FAR 6.303-1.

1806.303-170 Sole-source purchases by contractors.

The requirements of FAR Part 6 and NFS part 1806 apply if NASA directs a prime contractor (by specifications, drawings, parts lists, or otherwise) to purchase items on a sole-source basis. Accordingly, procurement officers shall take necessary actions to ensure that such sole-source acquisitions are properly justified.

1806.303-270 Use of unusual and compelling urgency authority.

(a) When using the authority of FAR 6.302-2, the justification required in FAR 6.303 shall describe and provide rationale as to the extent and nature of the harm to the Government by: quantifying the serious injury; estimating the cost and describing the basis for the estimate of the financial injury. If personal injury or loss of life or any other injury is probable, describe the circumstances behind this potential injury/loss and why no other action could avert these conditions. Include a chronological explanation of events that caused the urgent situation. The justification must also explain the extent to which competition is limited and describe the extent to which maximum practicable competition was obtained given the circumstances.

(b) If the authority at FAR 6.302-2 is used for extending the performance period of an existing services contract, the justification shall contain the information required by FAR 6.303-2 and;

(1) Documentation that the acquisition process for the successor contract was started early enough to allow for adequately planning and conducting a full and open competition, together with a description of the circumstances that prevented award in a timely manner; and

(2) Documentation of the reasons why no other source could practicably compete for the interim requirement.

1813.302-71 Policy.

(a) The NASA Shared Services Center (NSSC) is designated as the Agency's sole purchasing activity for the acquisition of all supplies and services valued at or below the simplified acquisition threshold (SAT), except for the following:

(1) Purchases made using the Government purchase card (see 1813.301), unless the purchase card function has been delegated to the NSSC.

(2) Indefinite delivery, indefinite quantity (IDIQ) contracts or blanket purchase agreements (BPAs) that permit the award of orders with a potential value over the SAT.

(3) Orders, regardless of value, awarded against IDIQ contracts or BPAs that have been retained by the center. This does not include orders issued against any of the Solutions for Enterprise-Wide Procurement (SEWP) contracts.

(4) Interagency Agreements.

(5) Orders for construction, facility repair or architect & engineering (A&E) services (Material Groups: C1, C2, Y, and Z).

(6) SAT purchases made by institutional support contractors on behalf of the Agency.

(b) Agency requiring activities shall use the Simplified Acquisition Customer Portal (SACP) to submit SAT requests to the NSSC for processing, tracking and award. The SACP is assessable via the NASA Enterprise Service Desk at https://esd.nasa.gov/esd. Materials pertaining to the use of the SACP, and other NSSC SAT guidance and procedures are located on the NSSC SAT webpage at URL: https://www.nssc.nasa.gov/simplifiedacquisition.

Office of Personnel Management Federal Employees Health Benefits Acquisition Regulation (FEHBAR)

PART 1606—COMPETITION REQUIREMENTS

Section Contents

Authority: 5 U.S.C. 8913; 40 U.S.C. 486(c); 48 CFR 1.301.

1606.001 Applicability.

FAR part 6 has no practical application to FEHBP contracts in view of the statutory exception provided by 5 U.S.C. 8902.

Chapter 8 - Write it for the Contracting Officer!

As a prior Contract Specialist and Contracting Officer writing the documentation is time consuming. There are so many documentations that a Contracting Specialist has to complete, get reviewed, and approved by the Contracting Officer and higher signature authorities. What can a contractor, vendor, or even business can do is have their documentation prepared. Answer the questions directly and not attempt to commit fraud or mislead.

The documentation that a contactor can have prepared are the following:

1. <u>Proprietary Letter</u> on a business letterhead is to certify a made, offered, or sold only under the exclusive rights of the property ownership (governed by copyright, patent, and trade secret laws) of a manufacturer, offeror, or seller. Proprietary

items usually have distinctive characteristics or features, and are often incompatible with competing items.

2. <u>License Agreement</u>. Many supplies or services are acquired subject to supplier license agreements. These are particularly common in information technology acquisitions, but they may apply to any supply or service.

   A licensing agreement is a legal contract between two parties, known as the licensor and the licensee. In a typical licensing agreement, the licensor grants the licensee the right to produce and sell goods, apply a brand name or trademark, or use patented technology owned by the licensor.

3. <u>Justification and Approval</u>. This is sole sourcing of using one of the exceptions outlined in Chapter 7 - Other Than Full and Open Competition also known As Sole Source Contracts or one of the Small Business Set-Asides that allows for sole sourcing. *Example and how to search is provided.*

4. <u>Determination of Fair and Reasonable</u> – Can be determined in two FAR Parts. FAR Subpart Part 13.106-3(a) and FAR Subpart 15.404-1 -- Proposal Analysis Techniques. Determination of Reasonable determines if the Government is purchasing is in fair to purchase with the tax payer dollar. To make sure that the Government is not getting ripped off. *Example Memorandums will be provided.*

5. <u>Determination of Responsibility</u> – Yes, the Contracting Officer has to do this, but by having it prepared, it help alleviate questions if the Contracting Officer or Specialist reaches out and questions your business being responsible. This financially, past performance, experience, etc. *Example Memorandums will be provided.*

What about this being falling under FAR -- Part 3 Improper Business Practices and Personal Conflicts of Interest?

- Reality it comes down to the Contracting Officer to accept the documentation and review. By providing the documentation your company is supporting the acquisition.

- These documents need completed before solicitation (propriety letter, licensing agreement, & justification and approval).

- Prior to award of the Contract Determination of Fair and Reasonable & Determination of Responsibility.

- The Contracting officer will determine if the documentation is valid. Or to not use it. Regardless the Contracting Officer has to make the determinations before award.

Recommendation: The GOLD is in the priority letter, licensing agreement, Justification and approval, and if your business is prepared to answer questions if questions come up for Determination of Responsibility.

The Government will not purchase from your company unless the Requiring Activity –an individual or a program office that is responsible for establishing the agencies need. The agencies need can be a supply, service to be performed, or a construction project. The requiring activity is the one that will develop the documentation needed for this requirement that the Government intends to purchase.

Every year around July the budget is reviewed for the next year and determinations may be made on what to purchase for the following fiscal year. In Chapter 2 – Market Research by pulling Historical Contract – www.usaspending.gov Your business can see everything being purchased in a city by state or by the Federal Government through analyzing the excel worksheet that is derived off of the search.

Instead of just sending out your capabilities statement; which goes in the trash majority of the time. Add the supporting documentation that will separate your company from others (Justification and Approval, but also Determination of Responsibility).

Justification and Approval Content

Below is what needs to be annotated in a Justification and Approval. If the information is not within the Justification and Approval, then it should be challenged. Contracting Officers will try to work around some of the documentation, but it is not valid. That is where you protest before award. You can protest the agency or the Government Accountability Office.

FAR Subpart 6.303-2 -- Content.

(a) Each justification shall contain sufficient facts and rationale to justify the use of the specific authority cited.

(b) As a minimum, each justification, except those for sole-source 8(a) contracts over $22 million (see paragraph (d) of this section), shall include the following information:

(1) Identification of the agency and the contracting activity, and specific identification of the document as a "Justification for other than full and open competition."

(2) Nature and/or description of the action being approved.

(3) A description of the supplies or services required to meet the agency's needs (including the estimated value).

(4) An identification of the statutory authority permitting other than full and open competition.

(5) A demonstration that the proposed contractor's unique qualifications or the nature of the acquisition requires use of the authority cited.

(6) A description of efforts made to ensure that offers are solicited from as many potential sources as is practicable, including whether a notice was or will be publicized as required by Subpart 5.2 and, if not, which exception under 5.202 applies.

(7) A determination by the contracting officer that the anticipated cost to the Government will be fair and reasonable.

(8) A description of the market research conducted (see Part 10 – Market Research) and the results or a statement of the reason market research was not conducted.

(9) Any other facts supporting the use of other than full and open competition, such as:

   (i) Explanation of why technical data packages, specifications, engineering descriptions, statements of work, or purchase descriptions suitable for full and open competition have not been developed or are not available.

   (ii) When 6.302-1 (Only One Responsible Source and No Other Supplies or Services Will Satisfy Agency Requirements) is cited for follow-on acquisitions as described in 6.302-1(a)(2)(ii) (duplication of cost), an estimate of the cost to the Government that would be duplicated and how the estimate was derived.

   (iii) When 6.302-2 (Unusual and Compelling Urgency) is cited, data, estimated cost, or other rationale as to the extent and nature of the harm to the Government.

(10) A listing of the sources, if any, that expressed, in writing, an interest in the acquisition.

(11) A statement of the actions, if any, the agency may take to remove or overcome any barriers to competition before any subsequent acquisition for the supplies or services required.

(12) Contracting officer certification that the justification is accurate and complete to the best of the contracting officer's knowledge and belief.

(c) Each justification shall include evidence that any supporting data that is the responsibility of technical or requirements personnel (*e.g.*, verifying the Government's minimum needs or schedule requirements or other rationale for other than full and open competition) and which form a basis for the justification have been certified as complete and accurate by the technical or requirements personnel.

(d) As a minimum, each justification for a sole-source 8(a) contract over $22 million shall include the following information:

(1) A description of the needs of the agency concerned for the matters covered by the contract.

(2) A specification of the statutory provision providing the exception from the requirement to use competitive procedures in entering into the contract (see 19.805-1 Competitive 8(a)).

(3) A determination that the use of a sole-source contract is in the best interest of the agency concerned.

(4) A determination that the anticipated cost of the contract will be fair and reasonable.

(5) Such other matters as the head of the agency concerned shall specify for purposes of this section.

Justification and Approval

Every agency has a Justification and Approval process. That is who signs and minuet differences in their Justification and Approval. Not all will look alike. The next example page will cover Searching for Justification and Approval Examples

See Next Page.

JUSTIFICATION & APPROVAL

FOR OTHER THAN FULL AND OPEN COMPETITION

TEMPLATE

DIRECTORATE OF CONTRACTING
Office of the Principal Assistant Responsible
For Contracting U.S. Army Corps of Engineers

DATE

JUSTIFICATION AND APPROVAL
FOR OTHER THAN FULL AND OPEN COMPETITION

1. **CONTRACTING AGENCY:** Specify the contracting agency responsible for this action.

2. **DESCRIPTION OF ACTION**: Describe the nature of the contractual action for which approval is requested (i.e., new contract, modification). Include contract type (i.e., FFP, CPAF etc.); and type and year of funds to be used (R&D, CIVIL WORKS, MILCON, OMA); and estimated share and ceiling arrangements, when applicable.

   a. For instance: "A new firm-fixed price contract citing FYxx OMA funds" OR: "A modification to cost plus fixed fee contract number W91xxx-07-C-0001, citing FYxx CIVIL WORKS funds."

   b. If the contract has option years, say something like: "... citing FYxx OMA funds for the base year, and FYxx thru FYxx OMA funds for each subsequent option year."

   c. If there are circumstances where more than one type of funds is cited, use paragraph 3, below, to describe the type and amount to be used for each part of the requirement.

3. **DESCRIPTION OF SUPPLIES/SERVICES OR NATURE OF CONSTRUCTION:**

Describe the supplies and/or services or construction to be acquired. Include quantities and/or the performance period, as well as the estimated total value (including options if any). See note (3)(d) below for a discussion of options when using Urgency as your exception).

   a. Briefly describe the supplies and/or services and/or construction -- it is neither desired nor required for detailed specifications or equipment lists to be included. Explain the requirement in nontechnical terms so it can be understood by a reviewer/auditor/member of the legal profession who is not familiar with the requiring activity or the requirement. If

257

the description of the type of supplies, construction and/or services is not readily understood, chances of repeated questioning or action disapproval are significantly increased. For examples, see sample J&As at the PARC website.

b. If the action described is a modification to an existing contract, be sure to distinguish clearly between the work covered by the basic contract and the additional work to be obtained by the proposed modification. It is also appropriate to explain why the modification is outside the scope of the contract vehicle.

c. Identify the requiring activity.

d. Option quantities and/or performance periods:

(1) If option quantities and/or performance periods are included in the contract, the value of each option must be shown separately, and included in the total estimated value of the J&A. It is also necessary to state whether options will be evaluated. (Note: If options are not priced and evaluated at time of contract award, a separate J&A must be approved before any option is exercised.)

(2) If FAR clauses 52.237-3 (Continuity of Services) and/or 52.217-8 (Option to Extend Services) will be included in your noncompetitive contract, be sure to mention each and its associated potential time period and dollar value. (These two clauses should be considered for inclusion in competitive contracts to preclude the necessity for later noncompetitive actions if the follow-on is delayed or if a phase-in/phase-out period is required.)

(3) If the J&A is based on Exception 2 (Unusual and Compelling Urgency), Option quantities and/or performance periods **should not** be included. The philosophy behind this is that an "Urgent" requirement should only be for the absolute minimum quantity/period. See GAO Decisions - Master Security, Inc., B-235711, Oct 4, 89, 89-2 CPD para. 303 and Colbar, Inc., B-230754, Jun 13, 88, 88-1 CPD para. 562. If options

are deemed necessary for an Urgent J&A, they need to be separately supported and justified.

(a) A notable exception to the philosophy above is the need for continued services/supplies using an interim contract or an extension to an existing contract when there is a protest prior to or upon award of the follow on contract. In this case, the J&A may be for a base period of ___ months (minimum time you expect resolution to take) plus a maximum of 3 one-month options. The J&A must specifically state that each option will be exercised only if resolution of the protest does not occur during the previous period. See Appendix A, below for specific information that must be included in these cases.

e. The amount shown in paragraph 3 of the J&A must be the same amount shown on the Justification Review Document. If the J&A is under Exception 2 (Urgency) and is submitted "after the fact," use the actual contract amount rather than the original estimate.

4. **AUTHORITY CITED**: Identify the statutory authority, FAR/DFARS citation and FAR/DFARS title permitting other than full and open competition.

For instance: "10 U.S.C. 2304(c)(1), as implemented by FAR 6.302-1 and DFARS 206.302-1, Only One Responsible Source". If the FAR contains subparagraphs describing different circumstances that may justify use of the authority you have cited, identify the appropriate subparagraphs, e.g., FAR 6.302-1(a)(2)(i) for unsolicited proposals (See Appendix A for additional information).

5. **REASON FOR AUTHORITY CITED:** Describe why the requirement necessitates invoking the authority cited. This is one of the key elements upon which approval is granted. Illustrate why the proposed acquisition MUST be accomplished through other than full and open competition, and why the authority in paragraph 4 applies. Provide a well-reasoned, detailed discussion of the requirement which will make it clear to someone who has never

heard of your organization or your requirement why full and open competition cannot be used for the procurement.

a. For clarity, divide paragraph 5 into subparagraphs rather than putting several unrelated thoughts together. Make an outline of the salient points which might harm the government (i.e. time, cost, life/safety, national security). Provide a topic sentence for each point and the supporting facts and logic behind it. Look to your market research to buoy assumptions and assertions. Although the guide at AR 25-50 was not written for J&As, you may use this to assist with proper paragraph structure and numbering.

b. Suggested paragraphs:

   (1) <u>Background:</u> Discuss the events/history/circumstances which lead to the use of procedures for other than full and open competition.

   (2) <u>Justification:</u>

      (a) What are the verified minimum requirements of the item/service/ construction? Include a discussion of the unique requirements of the item/ service/construction that necessitate a noncompetitive action. Describe how the required delivery/performance date impacted the decision to restrict competition. Bring out life/safety issue if applicable. If you are relying on assumptions rather than facts, i.e. *projected* cost based on parametric or historical data, please indicate as appropriate.

      (b) Identify the proposed sole source contractor (if applicable) and discuss the unique capabilities, experience, expertise, etc. that the contractor has that makes the firm the only one capable of performing the required work.

      (c) If competition was feasible had more time been available, discuss other factors that had an impact on the decision to solicit only one source to satisfy the requirement (i.e., cost/time to conduct a competitive procurement; time available versus time required; phase-in/phase-out time; complexity of requirement; etc.).

(d) If you indicate the required action was "directed or mandated" by someone, be sure to include full information saying **who** imposed the requirement (Rank or Title, authority as it relates to the procurement or program). Then provide a copy of the directive or mandate as an attachment to the J&A (letter, e-mail, etc.).

(e) Was the item or service previously acquired? If so, was it from the same contractor? If this is a continuation of a previous effort by the same contractor, discuss why no other sources of supply are available. Can alternate products or services be used and obtained competitively? If so, why is that alternative not being pursued?

(3) Impact: Fully describe the detrimental effects to the mission of the requiring activity or to the government which would result if this J&A was not approved and, consequently, the product, construction or service could not be provided. A general statement of mission failure is not sufficient. The statements must be able to pass the "So what?" test. Give specific examples of the nature and severity of the impact with dollar or other factors wherever possible.

(a) Do not cite conclusions (for example: "the government will be injured") without explaining the facts which form the basis of that conclusion. You must fully explain the reasons for the "injury" and why that "injury" cannot be tolerated. Describe life/safety issues, i.e., "failure to dredge the shoal immediately narrows the shipping channel with potential for collision and subsequent loss of life and property. The Coast Guard (Commander Justina Riley (912- 657-0098) received two complaints about vessels sheering to the right as they pass through Sections 2AA and AAB of the channel in the past week (July 15, 2008.)"

(b) Do not say "any delay will be costly" without explaining how it will be costly and what the cost impact will be. Use "actuals" for dollars or other resource impacts whenever possible.

(4) <u>Alternatives</u>: Discuss alternatives which were available to the government, reasons (technical, cost, etc.) why each was unacceptable except for the alternative selected, and the impact if other alternatives had been selected. Among the possible alternatives might be to (a) suspend operations, (b) use in-house personnel/expertise, (c) replace rather than upgrade an existing system (include costs already invested, training costs, and replacement costs if requested item is not received), etc. If there are similar products, describe the technical aspects of each and the decision making process used to determine that similar product(s) are not acceptable. Again, market research is invaluable to this discussion.

6. **EFFORTS TO OBTAIN COMPETITION:** Describe efforts made to ensure that offers are solicited from as many potential sources as is practicable. Also describe the extent of effective competition anticipated for this acquisition.

a. State when the requirement was synopsized (sources sought and/or regular) in the FedBizOpps and the number of responses received to the advertisement.

b. Use of Exception 2 (Urgency) requires soliciting as many sources as is practicable under the circumstances. State how many sources were solicited and how many offers were received.

c. If the J&A is for a contract modification, efforts to obtain competition on the original procurement should also be discussed.

d. Sometimes information in this paragraph and paragraph 8 (Market Survey) overlap. There is no need to restate the information -- just cross-reference the paragraphs.

e. If paragraph 5 fully explains why competition was not feasible for the particular action, you should include something like: "Based on information in paragraph 5, above, competition for this action was not feasible."

7. **ACTIONS TO INCREASE COMPETITION**: Include a statement of the actions taken (or to be taken) to increase competition before any subsequent acquisition of the supplies or services is required. There may be instances where it is not possible to compete the current acquisition; explain how competition will be increased or enhanced for the required supplies or services (to include breakout or other considerations). Consider some of the following: (a) May the item be redesigned such that it would enhance its ability to be competed in the future?; (b) Can the contractor be persuaded to provide the specifications, drawings, etc., which will enable the government to compete the item now or in the future?

   a. Another instance might be expressed: "The requiring activity is currently preparing specifications that will be adequate for full and open competition on a follow-on requirement anticipated for execution during FYxx. Market research will be performed for the follow-on requirement to identify all potential sources."

   b. If the current requirement is for an interim contract (or an extension of an existing contract), this paragraph could read something like: "Forty firms have requested a copy of the solicitation for the fully competitive follow-on requirement. To date, four offers have been received."

8. **MARKET RESEARCH:** Describe the extent of the market research (FAR 10.002) conducted to identify all qualified sources and the results thereof.

   a. Market research (see FAR 5.001, FAR 10.001, FAR 11.002, and DFARS 210.001) is the process of collecting and analyzing information on industry capabilities, interest and past performance in fulfilling the program statement of need/requirement. Market research must be conducted before developing each J&A and the information obtained from the market research results will be used by the J&A Project Delivery Team (PDT) to determine if sources capable of satisfying the agency's requirements exist. The PDT must not only consider market research to determine if a J&A is appropriate, but also have it address future needs. Consider if the market will be the same when this item/service/construction is procured again. How does the market assist the Government in providing maximum practicable opportunities in its acquisitions to Small Business, Service-Disabled Veteran-Owned Small Business, HUBZone business and Small Disadvantaged Business (see FAR 19.201, DFARS PGI 219.2). The market research should also answer the question - Can the procurement be restructured or the SOW/PWS revised to allow for full and open competition now or in the future? Techniques for conducting market research are contained under FAR 10.002.

b. Market research should be performed in a timely manner early in the acquisition process (prior to the preparation of a J&A) and tailored as appropriate to the goods or services being acquired. Market research has traditionally been the responsibility of technical personnel. However, since the contracting office more appropriately accomplishes some of the recommended techniques, market research should be conducted as a joint coordinated effort between the requiring activity and the contracting office to maximize results. Prior to contacting any potential sources, the requiring activity should discuss the proposed market research plan with the contracting officer to avoid any possible unauthorized vendor contacts or inadvertent release of advance acquisition information.

c. The intent of market research is to create or increase competition by locating and ensuring that all interested and capable sources are given the opportunity to compete for the goods and services to satisfy our minimum requirements. Competition should help the government receive the best value for its money. The J&A must include a detailed description and results of the market research or a statement discussing why it was not conducted. Absence of market research should be rare. When conducting Market Research, districts/centers should not request potential sources to submit more than the minimum information necessary (see FAR 10.001(b)). The District/Center's SBA Representative and Deputy for Small Business Programs should assist in determining what information will be required for submission by potential sources. In addition, the market research information may be supplemented by reviewing small business databases such as the SBA Dynamic Small Business Search engine located at: http://dsbs.sba.gov/dsbs/search/dsp_dsbs.cfm.

d. Be sure to include details of your market research: date conducted, name of person contacted, their title or role; organization; location; phone number, etc. Types of questions asked and responses. The intent is that your research may be easily duplicated. For example, if technology limits competition for fire alarm controllers in 2007 you may be able to go back to the same sources in 2008 to see what developments have been made in creating open architecture which would allow multiple firms' controllers. Even if systems are incompatible there may be a bridging or translation system which allows different components to communicate. What are the time and error rate in translation systems? A tenth of a second delay in a heating/cooling system may be acceptable. That may not be acceptable in a fire control system, for life safety reasons.

e. Try to break a system down to its smallest noncompetitive component. Unless justified, don't sole source the entire fire alarm system, just the controller which communicates with the fire station.

f. A "sources sought" synopsis is a valuable tool to determine whether sources other than the suggested sole source can satisfy the requirement. One advantage to this type of synopsis is that it can be issued as soon as the requirement becomes known. You do not have to wait until funds are provided or for the details of the procurement to be finalized. There is no set format for this type of synopsis as there is for a regular synopsis. You should include all known performance and/or technical information so contractors can determine whether they may be able to satisfy the requirement. The Special Competition Advocate (SCA) will be looking for "sources sought" efforts to be discussed in J&As.

g. The inadequacy of technical data is an unacceptable justification for poor market research techniques. The marketplace can sometimes be a better judge of the adequacy or even the necessity of technical data.

h. It is not acceptable to justify a sole source on the fact that a technical activity found a desirable product during market research (or an unofficial evaluation of available products) that has a lower price than others they reviewed. The process of finding the best product at the best cost must be left to the contracting officer.

i. The extent of time and effort involved in market research should be commensurate with the requirements, dollar value, and complexity of each procurement. However, repetitive procurement of the same or similar items should be considered when determining the level of effort necessary. Multiple buys within a year's period of the same item which can be predicted or reasonably projected based on programs or historical data should require enough research to support the aggregate.

k. There are no waivers available for market research. However, FAR Part 10 recognizes urgency and provides a requirement to perform market research based on "circumstances." That may result in an abbreviated market research based on readily available historical and commercial information. The magnitude of the research effort must be outlined as well as justification why the abbreviated research is adequate "for the circumstances." Performing solid easily replicated market research when time permits may aid in quickly updated research for emergency procurements.

9. **INTERESTED SOURCES:** Include a listing of the sources that expressed written interest In the acquisition.

a. If responses were received, discuss the content of the response and how the response was considered, further communication with responder, etc. If a response contained information sufficient to conduct a preliminary evaluation, you may say something like: "Preliminary technical information submitted by ABC Corp. in response to the FedBizOpps notice has been reviewed by the requiring activity who has advised that ABC does not appear to meet the requirements in the RFP." Or, perhaps: "... by the requiring activity who has advised that ABC Corp.'s product may be acceptable; however, final determination will be made after evaluation of ABC's formal proposal when submitted." In any case, a copy of the RFP must be provided to anyone responding to the FedBizOpps notice; if they submit a proposal, it must be considered.

b. If no responses were received, clearly state "To date, no other sources have expressed an interest in writing however, all offers received shall be considered." Also state that the notices required by FAR 5.201 shall be/have been published and any bids or proposals received shall be considered.

c. If industry responses only amounted to requests for the solicitation and no additional information was provided, say something like: "ABC Corp. and XYZ Co. requested copies of the RFP but provided no information to determine whether these firms can satisfy this requirement."

d. A Sources Sought in the Government Point of entry (GPE – FedBizOpps) and/or market research should be issued/conducted as soon as the requirement is known so contractors may respond while the J&A is being prepared. The Sources Sought and market research and their results must occur prior to processing the J&A in accordance with FAR 6.302-1(c)(2)).

e. If a GPE notice of intent will not be published, state which exception in FAR 5.202 applies. In all other instances a notice of intent should be placed in the GPE in addition to the Sources Sought in the GPE. If circumstances preclude even a Sources Sought, prior approval to omit GPE results must be obtained from the SCA prior to submitting the J&A for approval. For those urgent requirements not synopsized in the GPE, be sure to include the name of all offerors submitting a proposal. An offeror's address and amount of the offer are not required.

f. If additional responses are received after the J&A has been forwarded for approval that indicate other sources may be available, the contracting officer must submit updated information to the SCA. A memorandum may be used to forward the additional information (company name, date response was received, substance of the response, disposition or action taken).

g. Use of synopsis Note 22 does not negate the responsibility to provide a copy of the solicitation to potential competitors. It would be unreasonable to expect a contractor to submit a proposal without a copy of the solicitation that describes the required item/service.)

NOTE 22

"The proposed contract action is for supplies or services for which the Government intends to solicit and negotiate with only one source under the authority of FAR 6.302. Interested persons may identify their interest and capability to respond to the requirement or submit proposals. This notice of intent is not a request for competitive proposals. However, all proposals received within forty-five days (thirty days if award is issued under an existing basic ordering agreement) after date of publication of this synopsis will be considered by the Government." A determination by the Government not to compete with this proposed contract based upon responses to this notice is solely within the discretion of the Government. Information received will normally be considered solely for the purpose of determining whether to conduct a competitive procurement."

10. OTHER FACTORS: Discuss any other factors supporting the use of other than full and open competition, such as:

a. Procurement history. The following items of information are expected.

(1) Contract numbers and dates of the last several awards that are recent and pertinent to this acquisition.

(2) Competitive status of these actions.

(3) Authority for less than full and open competition previously used.

(4) If a J&A was prepared to support the immediately prior buy, briefly describe the Actions to Increase Competition (paragraph 7) mentioned in that prior J&A, and explain the results thereof.

(5) If any prior award was accomplished by full and open competition, explain the changed circumstances in detail.

(6) Explain any unusual patterns that may be revealed by the history, e.g., several consecutive, urgent buys.

b. Reasonable efforts to retrieve required information are expected. Resources include past contract files, and the Field/Special Competition Advocate management files.

c. Causes for Delay in the Acquisition Process: Explain why technical data packages, specifications, engineering descriptions, statements of work or purchase descriptions suitable for full and open competition have not been developed or are not available. Describe actions taken or planned to remedy this situation, unless otherwise covered in a previous section.

NOTE: If not available, are any of these being developed? If not, why not? How much lead time would be required to develop it? Has any cost-benefit analysis been conducted to determine whether it is advantageous to the government to buy or develop it? If not, what evidence is available to demonstrate why analysis is not needed? Some type of specification, work statement, or description must be prepared even if the procurement is sole source.

d. If a requirement for first article testing is the principal reason for not awarding the contract on a full and open basis, clearly describe the reasons that first article testing is required on this procurement and why other means of assuring quality are not being used.

NOTE: Although the AFARS format instructions state that information concerning injury to the government should be shown in paragraph 10, it is more appropriate to include this information in the justification required by paragraph 5. There is no need to duplicate this information in paragraph 10, just say "See paragraph 5, above."

    e. Subcontracting Competition: In single source situations, address efforts to be taken by the government to assure that the prime contractor obtains as much competition as possible in its subcontracting.

11. **TECHNICAL CERTIFICATION:**

"I certify that the supporting data under my cognizance which are included in the J&A are accurate and complete to the best of my knowledge and belief."

NAME: _____   DATE: _____

TITLE: _____   SIGNATURE: _____

12. **REQUIREMENTS CERTIFICATION:**

"I certify that the supporting data under my cognizance which are included in the J&A are accurate and complete to the best of my knowledge and belief."

NAME: _____   DATE: _____

TITLE: _____   SIGNATURE: _____

13. **FAIR AND REASONABLE COST DETERMINATION:**

"I hereby determine that the anticipated cost for this contract action will be fair and reasonable." Or, for those J&As citing Exception 2 (Urgency), submitted after award: "... that the cost for this contract action was fair and reasonable." Provide the basis for this determination (e.g., describe techniques used or to be used to determine fair and reasonable price, such as cost analysis, price analysis, audit, should cost, independent government estimate, etc.).

NAME: _____   DATE: _____

TITLE: Contracting Officer   SIGNATURE: _____

14. CONTRACTING OFFICER CERTIFICATION:

"I certify that this J&A is accurate and complete to the best of my knowledge and belief."

NAME: _____   DATE: _____

TITLE: <u>Contracting Officer</u>   SIGNATURE: _____

(Put the approval paragraph on a separate page.)

<u>APPROVAL</u>

Based on the foregoing justification, I hereby approve the procurement **of** *(the short title of the supplies and/or services being procured; should be similar to "Program/Equipment" on the Justification Review Document.)* on an other than full and open competition basis pursuant to the authority of 10 U.S.C. 2304(c)( ) *(the appropriate exception to full and open competition goes into this space; it should agree with the Justification Review Document and paragraph 4 of the J&A),* subject to the availability of funds, and provided the *(fill in either "property," "services," or "property and services.")* herein described (have/has) otherwise been authorized for acquisition.

NAME: _____   DATE: _____

TITLE: _____   SIGNATURE: _____

Searching for Justification and Approval Examples

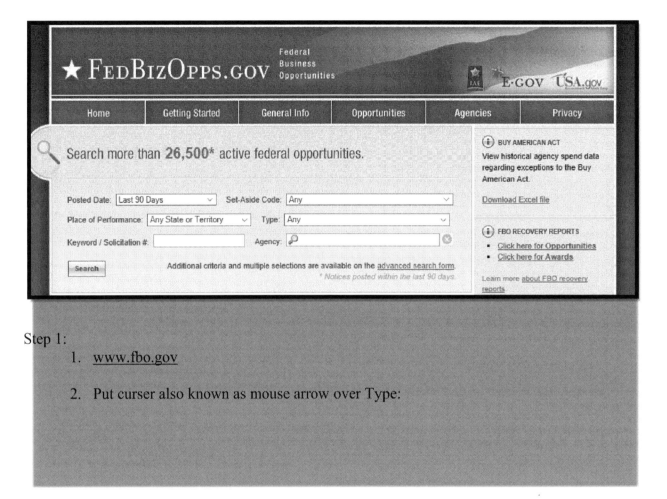

Step 1:

1. www.fbo.gov

2. Put curser also known as mouse arrow over Type:

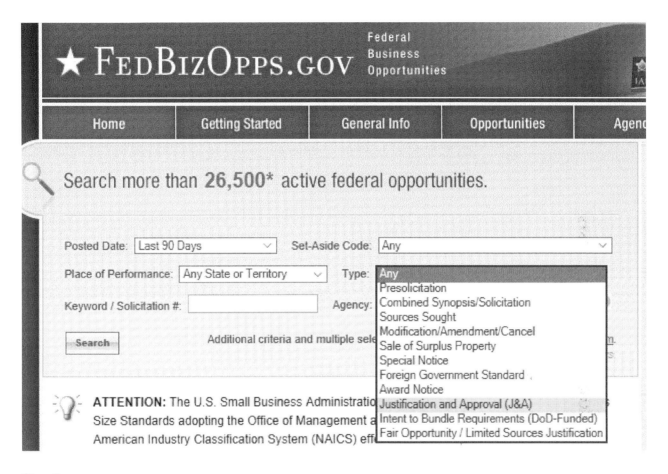

Step 2:

1. Put curser also known as mouse arrow over Type

2. Scroll down to Justification and Approval (J&A)

3. Hit search.

   Note: Variations of posted date, place of performance, key words, set-aside, and even
   agencies can be completed for more specifics.

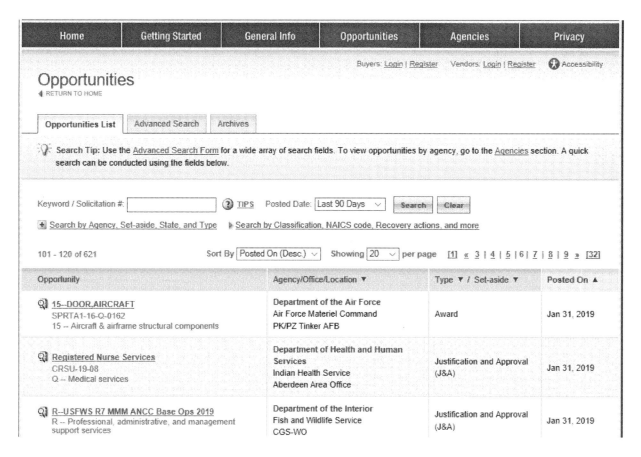

Step 3:

    1.   Select the Opportunity to review.

    2.   For this example, R--USFWS R7 MMM ANCC Base Ops 2019.

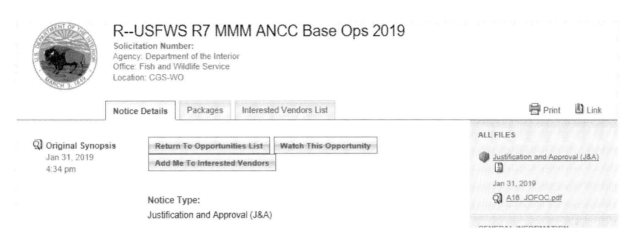

Step 4:
    1.   On the right side All Files, use the mouse to select A16JOFOC.PDF.

Step 5:
    1.   At the bottom of the page tap Open with the curser/mouse.

Determination of Fair and Reasonable

Each agency may use a different template. Some use a memorandum, others may have a form.

OFFICE LETTER HEAD

OFFICE SYMBOL **DATE**

MEMORANDUM FOR: Contracting Division, Paperless Contract Files

SUBJECT: Fair and Reasonable – **TITLE**

1. IAW FAR Subpart 15.404-1(b)(2) – Price analysis for commercial and non-commercial items. The Government may use various price analysis techniques and procedures to ensure a fair and reasonable price. Examples of such techniques include, but are not limited to the following: (*Check box that is applicable, explain in 2.*)

   ☐(i) Comparison of proposed prices received in response to the solicitation. Normally, adequate price competition establishes a fair and reasonable price (see 15.403-1(c)(1)(i)).

   ☐(ii) Comparison of proposed prices to historical prices paid, whether by the Government or other than the Government, for the same or similar items. This method may be used for commercial items including those "of a type" or requiring minor modifications.

   (A) The prior price must be a valid basis for comparison. If there has been a significant time lapse between the last acquisition and the present one, if the terms and conditions of the acquisition are significantly different, or if the reasonableness of the prior price is uncertain, then the prior price may not be a valid basis for comparison.

(B) The prior price must be adjusted to account for materially differing terms and conditions, quantities and market and economic factors. For similar items, the contracting officer must also adjust the prior price to account for material differences between the similar item and the item being procured.

(C) Expert technical advice should be obtained when analyzing similar items, or commercial items that are "of a type" or requiring minor modifications, to ascertain the magnitude of changes required and to assist in pricing the required changes.

☐(iii) Use of parametric estimating methods/application of rough yardsticks (such as dollars per pound or per horsepower, or other units) to highlight significant inconsistencies that warrant additional pricing inquiry.

☐(iv) Comparison with competitive published price lists, published market prices of commodities, similar indexes, and discount or rebate arrangements.

☐(v) Comparison of proposed prices with independent Government cost estimates.

☐(vi) Comparison of proposed prices with prices obtained through market research for the same or similar items.

☐(vii) Analysis of data other than certified cost or pricing data (as defined at 2.101) provided by the offeror.

2. Supporting factors of check box above is:

3. Point of contact for this memorandum can be reached at <u>E-MAIL</u> or (###) ###-####.

Prepared by:

John Doe
Contract Specialist

Approved by:

Jane Doe
Contracting Officer

Determination of Responsibility

Each agency may use a different template. Some use a memorandum, others may have a form.

OFFICE LETTER HEAD

OFFICE SYMBOL   **DATE**

MEMORANDUM FOR: Contracting Division, Paperless Contract Files

<u>**Determination and Findings**</u>

1. Determination and Findings will annotate the standards as an alpha character followed with a bullet determine if the vendor is responsive or non-responsive.

2. IAW FAR Subpart 9.104-1 to Determine a responsible, a prospective contractor must

   (a) Have adequate financial resources to perform the contract, or the ability to obtain them (see 9.104-3(a));

   - The vendor has performed **(# of Contracts)** firm-fixed-price contracts with the Federal Government and has performed various sub-contracts with the Government and Commercial sector. The vendor has the capable resources to perform the contract in accordance to their Contract Action Report in FPDS is that **(# of)** employees with an annual revenue of **($____._____)**. Responsive.

   (b) Be able to comply with the required or proposed delivery or performance schedule, taking into consideration all existing commercial and governmental business commitments.

   - Vendor proposed the pricing and schedule. Nothing deems that the vendor would be nonresponsive IAW to what has been proposed. Responsive.

(c) Have a satisfactory performance record (see 9.104-3(b) and Subpart 42.15). A prospective contractor shall not be determined responsible or non-responsible solely on the basis of a lack of relevant performance history, except as provided in 9.104-2;

- Market Research shows historical performance is satisfactory on the following contracts and FAPIIS that were awarded to **(Business Name)**

Annotate Contract History Here

(d) Have a satisfactory record of integrity and business ethics (for example, see Subpart 42.15);

- FAPIIS data was pulled on **Date** at **Time** and annotates zero records of dissatisfaction. Responsive.

(FAPIIS can be pulled from here <u>www.fapiis.gov</u>)

FAPIIS Data	Records	Count
Administrative Agreement	No	0
Defective Pricing	No	0
DoD Determination of Contractor Fault	No	0
Information on Trafficking in Persons	No	0
Non-Responsibility Determination	No	0
Recipient Not-Qualified Determination	No	0
Subcontractor Payment Issues	No	0
Termination for Cause	No	0
Termination for Default	No	0
Termination for Material Failure to Comply	No	0

(e) Have the necessary organization, experience, accounting and operational controls, and technical skills, or the ability to obtain them (including, as appropriate, such elements as production control procedures, property control systems, quality assurance measures, and safety programs applicable to materials to be produced or services to be performed by the prospective contractor and subcontractors). (See 9.104-3 (a).)

- See bullet (a) – Responsive.

(f) Have the necessary production, construction, and technical equipment and facilities, or the ability to obtain them (see 9.104-3(a)); and

- See bullet (a) – Responsive.

(g) Be otherwise qualified and eligible to receive an award under applicable laws and regulations (see also inverted domestic corporation prohibition at 9.108).

- System for Award Management was pulled on **Date** and review of FAR Provision 52.212-3 revealed that the vendor is not an Inverted Domestic Corporation.

(n) Prohibition on Contracting with Inverted Domestic Corporations.

(1) Government agencies are not permitted to use appropriated (or otherwise made available) funds for contracts with either an inverted domestic corporation, or a subsidiary of an inverted domestic corporation, unless the exception at 9.108-2(b) applies or the requirement is waived in accordance with the procedures at 9.108-4.

(2) Representation. the offeror represents that-

(i) It ☐ is, ☑ is not an inverted domestic corporation; and

(ii) It ☐ is, ☑ is not a subsidiary of an inverted domestic corporation.

- System for Award Management was pulled on **Date** to validate. No changes occurred. Responsive.

3. It is here determined IAW FAR Subpart 9.104-1 that:

Business information here

Is responsible for the award of the **(contract pricing type) (Contract type – Contract, Delivery Order, Task order, Purchase Order, etc.) (Task Order #)** written of off the base contract **(Contract #)** in response to **(Solicitation #)** in the amount of **($____._____)**.

4. Point of contact for this memorandum can be reached **(Contract Specialist or Contracting Officer)** or **(E-mail and Phone Number).**

Prepared by:

John Doe
Contract Specialist

Approved by:

Jane Doe
Contracting Officer

Chapter 9 – Recommendation & Closing

When it comes to Government Acquisitions or selling to the Government there is no guarantee that a vendor/business/contractor will win a Government Contract. The intent of Government Acquisition in creating a solicitation is to be fair. To allow maximum competition. Does this always occur? The answer is "No." However, the Government does allow Other than Full and Open Competition also known as sole sourcing. By knowing where to go in the FAR such as FAR Part 6 and parts of FAR Part 13 annotated in Chapter 7 - Other Than Full and Open Competition also known As Sole Source Contracts. The key points to remember:

1. The fiscal triad and the separation of powers are now know. That your business will barely get in front of the person that you need too.

2. Picking up the phone may help, but there is little that your business can do, because of the separations of power and the process it takes to be awarded a contract.

3. That the Government has the Competition in Contracting Act (CICA); but there are exceptions.

4. Back Room Deals can land your "inside person" with civil & criminal fines. This also can land your business with civil and criminal fines, but also suspension and debarment.

5. It does not matter who you know. They cannot guarantee you a contract!!

6. Stop E-mailing your business's capabilities statement to Government Contract Specialist and Contracting Officers.

7. If your business is an 8(a); e-mail away.

8. Look at teaming with 8(a) businesses. Be capable to perform IAW to FAR Clause 52.219-14 Limitations on Subcontracting; which should be in every solicitation and contracts for supplies, services, and construction, if any portion of the requirement is to be set aside or reserved for small business and the contract amount is expected to exceed $150,000. (This should be changing to $250,000).

a. Services (except construction). At least 50 percent of the cost of contract performance incurred for personnel shall be expended for employees of the concern.

b. Supplies (other than procurement from a nonmanufacturer of such supplies). The concern shall perform work for at least 50 percent of the cost of manufacturing the supplies, not including the cost of materials.

c. General construction. The concern will perform at least 15 percent of the cost of the contract, not including the cost of materials, with its own employees.

d. Construction by special trade contractors. The concern will perform at least 25 percent of the cost of the contract, not including the cost of materials, with its own employees.

9. Search for 8(a) through www.sam.gov, www.usaspending.gov, and http://dsbs.sba.gov/dsbs/search/dsp_dsbs.cfm

a. This same information can be used to find out who is purchasing your supplies, services, or construction.

b. It can help you find local federal agencies and what they purchase.

c. It will help you develop past pricing.

10. Look into becoming apart or partnering with a company in the Department of Defense Pilot Mentor-Protégé Program.

11. Knowing that set-asides and their potential of what can be sole sourced as HUBZone, WOSB, EDWOSB, SDVOSB, & VOSB. That this applies when the authority may be used when statutes, such as the following, expressly authorize or require that acquisition be made from a specified source.

Before considering a small business set-aside, provided none of the exclusions at FAR Subpart 19.1304

The Requirements that can be satisfied through award to:

I. Federal Prison Industries, Inc. https://www.unicor.gov/index.aspx

II. AbilityOne - https://www.abilityone.gov/procurement_list/index.html

III. Order under Agency Indefinite-delivery Contracts

IV. Federal Supply Schedules
https://www.gsaadvantage.gov/advantage/main/start_page.do

V. Requirements being completed by 8(a) participants

VI. Requirements that do not exceed the micro-purchase threshold (Can be purchased with a Government Purchase Card aka Credit Card)

   a. Construction - $2,000

   b. Services - $2,500

   c. Supplies- $10,000

VII. Requirements for commissary or exchange resale items.

VIII. The contracting officer does not have a reasonable expectation that offers would be received from two or more (*insert set-aside here*) owned small business concerns;

12. <u>Proprietary Letter</u> on a business letterhead is to certify a made, offered, or sold only under the exclusive rights of the property ownership (governed by copyright, patent, and trade secret laws) of a manufacturer, offeror, or seller. Proprietary items usually have distinctive characteristics or features, and are often incompatible with competing items.

13. <u>License Agreement</u>. Many supplies or services are acquired subject to supplier license agreements. These are particularly common in information technology acquisitions, but they may apply to any supply or service.

    A licensing agreement is a legal contract between two parties, known as the licensor and the licensee. In a typical licensing agreement, the licensor grants the licensee the right to produce and sell goods, apply a brand name or trademark, or use patented technology owned by the licensor.

14. Your Business now knows about Unsolicited Proposals, which are highly technical and unique.

15. The hidden world of the following areas to compete for acquisitions:
    a. Board Agency Announcements
    b. Small Business Innovation Research Topics.
    c. Small Business Technology Transfer Research Topics.
    d. Program Research and Development Announcements.

16. What needs to be in the Justification and Approvals; how to search for examples and have an example provided.

17. That the following are Circumstances Permitting Other Than Full and Open Competition by the Government:

a. Only One Responsible Source and No Other Supplies or Services Will Satisfy Agency Requirements.

b. Unusual and Compelling Urgency.

c. Industrial Mobilization; Engineering, Developmental, or Research Capability; or Expert Services.

d. International Agreement.

e. Authorized or Required by Statute.

f. National Security.

g. Public Interest.

18. That the following Government agencies have additional Circumstances Permitting Other Than Full and Open Competition:

a. Broadcasting of Governors - Notwithstanding these authorities, USAGM voluntarily follows the FAR in the conduct of most of its procurements, but reserves its right to exercise its authorities in those instances when competition poses severe challenges to the agency due to factors, such as geographical remoteness, uniqueness of requirement, requirements for unique skillsets, type of agreement, lack of public policy benefit, and other complexities related to the a fore listed.

b. Department of Agriculture Acquisition Regulation - Section 1472 of the National Agricultural Research, Extension, and Teaching Policy Act of 1977 (7 U.S.C. 3318) (the Act) authorizes the Secretary of Agriculture to award contracts, without competition, to further research, extension, or teaching programs in the food and agricultural sciences. The use of this authority is limited to those instances where it can be determined that contracting without full and open competition is in the best interest of the

Government and necessary to the accomplishment of the research, extension, or teaching program.

c. <u>Department of Commerce Acquisition Regulation</u> - In accordance with Executive Order 13457, a sole source acquisition may not be justified on the basis of any earmark included in any non-statutory source, except when otherwise required by law or when an earmark meets the criteria for funding set out in Executive Order 13457.

d. <u>Department of Education Acquisition Regulation</u> - May incrementally conduct successive procurements of modules of overall systems. Each module must be useful in its own right or useful in combination with the earlier procurement modules

e. <u>Department of Energy Acquisition Regulation</u> - Contracts for electric power or energy, gas (natural or manufactured), water, or other utility services when such services are available from only one source.

f. <u>Department of Health and Human Services Acquisition Regulation</u> - For acquisitions covered by 42 U.S.C. 247d-6a(b)(2)(A), "available from only one responsible source" shall be deemed to mean "available from only one responsible source or only from a limited number of responsible sources" and for medical drugs, devices, or to diagnose, mitigate, prevent, or treat harm from biological, chemical, radiological, or nuclear warfare, and technology that enhances the use or effect of a drug, biological product or device.

g. <u>Department of Homeland Security Acquisition Regulation</u> - during a declared disaster to sole source up to 150 days and local area set-aside.

h.   Department of Labor Acquisition Regulation - contracts for advisory and assistance services or for research and development, the contracting officer has the authority below the simplified acquisition threshold to approve sole source contracts.

i.   Department of State Acquisition Regulation - Department of State standardization program & local security guards.

j.   Department of Veterans Affairs Acquisition Regulation – verified SDVOSB or VOSB.

k.   Environmental Protection Agency Acquisition Regulation - The contracting officer may use other than full and open competition to acquire the services of experts for use in preparing or prosecuting a civil or criminal action under SARA whether or not the expert is expected to testify at trial. The contracting officer need not prepare the written justification under FAR 6.303 when acquiring expert services under the authority of section 109(e) of SARA. The contracting officer shall document the official contract file when using this authority.

l.   Office of Personnel Management Federal Employees' Life Insurance Federal Acquisition Regulation - FAR part 6 has no practical application to the FEGLI Program because 5 U.S.C. chapter 87 exempts the FEGLI Program from competitive bidding.

m.   National Aeronautics and Space Administration Federal Acquisition Regulations Supplement - NASA Shared Services Center (NSSC) is designated as the Agency's sole purchasing activity for the acquisition of all supplies and services valued at or below the simplified acquisition threshold (SAT).

 n. <u>Office of Personnel Management Federal Employees Health Benefits Acquisition Regulation</u> - FAR part 6 has no practical application to FEHBP contracts in view of the statutory exception provided by 5 U.S.C. 8902.

19. As a business when you go into negotiations it is about the Government determining Fair and Reasonable. If you know this, then you can be prepared to support that determination.

20. Finally can the Government determine your business responsible? You now know what the Government does to determine this. Success isn't far.

<u>Your company now knows the</u> <u>Secrets to Noncompetitive Government Contract!</u>

<u>Good Luck!</u>

References

Acquisition Regulations & Policies - www.acquisition.gov

Acquisition Regulations & Policies - http://farsite.hill.af.mil/

Contract Administration - https://www.sba.gov/partners/contracting-officials/contract-administration

DFARS Appendix GG - http://farsite.hill.af.mil/reghtml/regs/other/afars/GG_27_01.htm

Department of Labor Procurement Review Board https://www.dol.gov/oasam/boc/oams/prb.htm

Executive Order 13457—Protecting American Taxpayers From Government Spending on Wasteful Earmarks https://www.govinfo.gov/content/pkg/FR-2008-02-01/pdf/08-483.pdf

FedBid now known as Unison Marketplace – reverse auction https://www.unisonglobal.com/product-suites/acquisition/sourcing/marketplace/

Federal Contractor Misconduct Database (FCMD) https://www.contractormisconduct.org/about-fcmd

Federal Prison Industries – https://www.unicor.gov/index.aspx

Government Point of Entry – www.fbo.gov

Government Spending - www.usaspending.gov

Government Supply Schedule www.gsaadvantage.gov

GSA Advantage - https://www.gsaadvantage.gov/advantage/main/start_page.do

Interagency Contract Directory (ICD) - https://www.contractdirectory.gov/contractdirectory/

Integrity Lion Acquisitions, LLC - www.integritylionacq.com

List of Declarations - http://www.fema.gov/news/disasters.fema#sev2

Mentor-Protégé Program (MPP) - https://business.defense.gov/Programs/Mentor-Protégé -Program/

MP5301.601(a)(i) – Head of the Contracting Activity (HCA) Matrix - http://farsite.hill.af.mil/reghtml/regs/far2afmcfars/af_afmc/affars/MP5301.601(a)(i).htm

NASA Enterprise Service Desk - https://esd.nasa.gov/esd.

NSSC SAT webpage at URL - https://www.nssc.nasa.gov/simplifiedacquisition.

Small Business Contracting Goals - https://www.sba.gov/document/support--agency-contracting-goals

Small Business Dynamic Search - http://dsbs.sba.gov/dsbs/search/dsp_dsbs.cfm

Small Business Innovation Research Topics – https://www.sbir.gov/sbirsearch/topic/current

System for Award Management - www.sam.gov

U.S. Ability One Commission – https://www.abilityone.gov/procurement_list/index.html

Small Business Technology Transfer Research Topics

Department of Defense - https://sbir.defensebusiness.org/?AspxAutoDetectCookieSupport=1

Department of Energy – https://science.energy.gov/sbir/

Department of Health and Human Services – https://sbir.nih.gov/

National Aeronautics and Space Administration – https://sbir.gsfc.nasa.gov/

National Science Foundation – https://seedfund.nsf.gov/

Program Research and Development Announcements https://www.energy.gov/eere/ssl/research-development

Index

H

I

J

K

L

M

N

Made in the USA
Columbia, SC
12 February 2021